Romantic Days and Nights

in Savannah

Help Us Keep This Guide Up to Date

Every effort has been made by the authors and editors to make this guide as accurate and useful as possible. However, many things can change after a guide is published—establishments close, phone numbers change, facilities come under new management, and so on.

We would love to hear from you concerning your experiences with this guide and how you feel it could be made better and be kept up to date. While we may not be able to respond directly to your comments and suggestions, we'll take them to heart, and we'll be certain to share them with the author. Please send your comments and suggestions to the following address:

The Globe Pequot Press
Reader Response/Editorial Department
P.O. Box 480
Guilford, CT 06437

Or you may e-mail us at:
editorial@globe-pequot.com

Thanks for your input,
and happy travels!

Romantic Days and Nights®

IN SAVANNAH

Romantic Diversions In and Around the City

SECOND EDITION

by Georgia R. Byrd

The
Globe
Pequot
Press

GUILFORD, CONNECTICUT

Text design and cover illustration by M. A. Dubé.
Illustrations on pages 3, 14, 73, 80, and 133 by Lana Mullen. All others
    by M. A. Dubé.
Spot art by www.ArtToday.com.
Maps by Mary Ballachino.

Romantic Days and Nights is a registered trademark of The Globe Pequot Press.

Library of Congress Cataloging-in-Publication Data

Byrd, Georgia R.
    Romantic days and nights in Savannah : romantic diversions in and around the
  the city / by Georgia R. Byrd. -- 2nd ed.
      p. cm. -- (Romantic days and nights series)
    Includes index.
    ISBN 0-7627-0841-7
    1. Savannah Region (Ga.)--Guidebooks. 2. Couples--Travel--Georgia--Savannah
  Region--Guidebooks. I. Title. II. Series.
F294.S2 B97 2001
917 .58'7240444--dc21   00-066270

Manufactured in the United States of America
Second Edition/First Printing

This book is dedicated to my loving family—
my parents, John and Ann Rogers,
my children, Ammie and Whit Whitley,
and my husband, Joseph, who showed me how truly
romantic Savannah could be.

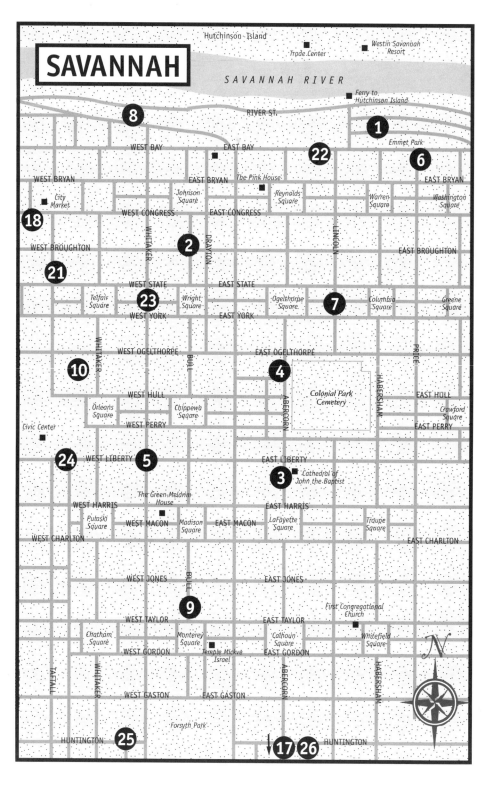

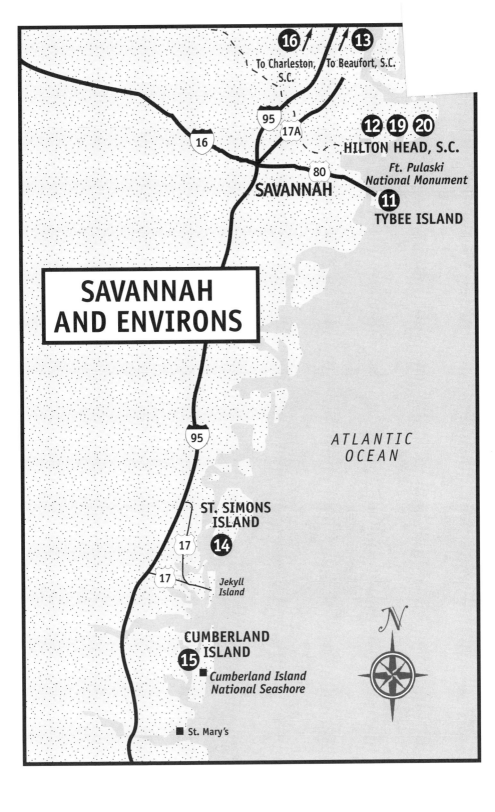

Contents

The prices and rates listed in this guidebook were confirmed at press time. We recommend, however, that you call establishments before traveling to obtain current information.

Acknowledgments

MANY THANKS TO Jenny Stacy of the Savannah Area Convention and Visitors Bureau, Eugene Downs, the Georgia Historical Society, and my family for their constant guidance and encouragement.

Introduction

BEYOND THE GRACEFUL CABLE-SPAN BRIDGE that crosses the winding Savannah River and connects South Carolina to Georgia, the city of Savannah unfurls flirtatiously like Scarlett O'Hara greeting her suitors. Crowned with a solid-gold dome, Savannah is adorned with towering church spires, ornate ironworks, and Roman arches. The city's extravagant buffet of architectural brilliance, Southern haute cuisine, and enchanting accommodations is a feast for lovers hungry for tranquillity.

For generations, beautiful Savannah has inspired poets, playwrights, and composers. More recently, the city's rich history has been recaptured in part by authors and screenwriters. Regardless of the reasons for its fame, however, Savannah is a city bred for passion.

British general James Oglethorpe founded Savannah in 1733 with a greatly heralded city plan that placed twenty-four orderly squares at regular intervals on a bluff overlooking the river. Designed to promote quaint meeting places for townspeople (and, coincidentally, scenic backdrops for both lovers and the lovelorn), the squares also created an enticing atmosphere, as the bakeries bordering them scented the streets with the heavenly aroma of freshly baked bread.

Today those squares still provide an intimate ambience unmatched by other American cities. Citizens and visitors alike choose midday picnic spots within the squares' boundaries. In summer, musicians perform on monument steps for passersby. Couples nestle on benches shaded by live oak trees laced with Spanish moss. Horse-drawn carriages click past the squares, sometimes carrying brides and grooms to historic churches. Walled gardens of nearby homes, museums, and restaurants hint at hidden delights. These images offer only a taste of Savannah's pleasures. Within and surrounding the city's 2.5-square-mile Historic District, a captivating kaleidoscope of fanciful pastimes is intermingled with intriguing tales and colorful characters. As if this seaside city weren't filled with enough treasures, just across the Savannah River lies a new jewel called Hutchinson Island. From undeveloped, unsightly land, where the gallant once braved mosquitoes and weeds in search of arrowheads and sharks' teeth, a new waterfront resort has arisen, one that adds a whole new dimension to Savannah's riverfront. Across the narrow Savannah River, literally just feet from the city's famous River Street, this new "Land of Oz" has redefined the trip to Savannah. Now couples who partake of the shops, pubs, and restaurants along the riverfront will be tempted to stay an extra day or two just to explore the other side—an oasis where they can be pampered in a world-famous spa, bask in the sun, or stroll a waterfront that reflects the historic city in all her splendor. The Westin Savannah Harbor Resort towers above an eighteen-hole golf course anchored in a setting of dense tropical foliage and abundant wildlife. As grand yachts hug the marina and colorful water ferries journey back and forth across the river, it becomes evident that Savannah and her new island friend simply exude romance.

The Itineraries

If you approach Savannah from the west after traveling the monotonous, pine-lined stretch of I–16 between Macon and the highway's dead-end in Savannah, you'll find yourself somewhat suddenly in the midst of a lavishly beautiful cityscape. Lush and picturesque in all seasons, Savannah seems made for love.

A charming blend of splendor and whimsy, order and extravagance, Savannah encourages both sophisticated romance and playful adventure. Designed to create compact, cozy interludes of both types amid a background of Southern hospitality, these itineraries will take you deep inside Savannah's heart. Most include activities for one- and two-day trips that can be enjoyed on either weekends or weekdays—Savannah is an all-day, every day, yearlong attraction.

Using This Book

Event dates and room or meal rates were accurate at press time but are, of course, subject to change. Room rates, for instance, are typically higher during festival weekends. The room prices stated in this guide are an average computed from the highest and lowest rates charged throughout the year. Whether you're planning to stay at one of more than fifty quaint inns (ranging from $89 to $450 per night) or at a moderately priced hotel chain in the city's midtown ($50 to $130), availability as well as price varies with the season. Fall and spring are busiest. Avoid disappointment by calling ahead to make reservations. You can call the accommodations listed in this guide directly, or contact the free reservations service of the **Savannah Area Convention and Visitors Bureau** at (877) SAVANNAH (728–2662).

Savannah offers hundreds of wonderful eateries ranging in style from soulful Southern cuisine to a type of gourmet cooking labeled "regional Southern cuisine" (typically Southern foods presented in artful combinations). Lunch and dinner prices quoted in this guidebook do not include tax, tip, drinks, or desserts (unless stated otherwise). "Expensive" means $50 or more per person for dinner and $25 for lunch; "moderate" means $25 per person for dinner and $15 per person for lunch; and "inexpensive" means $15 for dinner and $10 for lunch.

Speaking of inexpensive, the budget icon (look for the piggy bank in the margins) indicates less expensive hotel, restaurant, and entertainment alternatives.

On weekdays, travelers will find better rates in hotels and inns and shorter lines at popular eateries. Be aware that lunch crowds start gathering at favorite restaurants at nearly noon each day, so you are most likely to be seated with no wait if you arrive by 11:30 A.M. Dinnertime eating habits are similar, as Savannahians are creatures of habit: Drinks start at 5:00 P.M. and dinner by 7:00. If you dine early (at 5:30) or late (after 9:00), you'll enjoy a serene meal with little or no wait. Nearly all members of the hospitality industry here will echo similar sentiments regarding lodging and dining reservations: Make them *early*—especially in spring, when flowers are blooming, or during holiday or festival weekends.

GETTING HERE AND GETTING AROUND

The Savannah seduction begins instantly where the boredom of I–16 empties into the Southern oasis of Savannah's refined Historic District. The most common driving route to the city from the north or south is I–95, from which you will take I–16 (which runs west to east) downtown. You can also reach the city on U.S. 17, called the Ocean or Coastal Highway, which runs north to south through Savannah.

Located at exit 18A off I–95, **Savannah International Airport** is 16 miles from downtown Savannah and offers daily nonstop flights to major U.S. cities, including Chicago, Dallas, Houston, Miami, Washington, D.C., and New York, and convenient connecting

Ten Ways to Inspire Romance
in and around Savannah

1. Picnic under the shady live oaks at pretty Daffin Park.

2. Watch the shrimp boats come in at sunset on the Thunderbolt shore.

3. Stroll through antiques shops that line the city's streets.

4. Hop aboard a horse-drawn carriage for a leisurely, private ride through the Historic District.

5. Sample the sweets on River Street—from Savannah pralines to chocolate fudge.

6. Sip a late-night toddy at an intimate basement cafe.

7. Glide through the salt-marsh creeks of Tybee Island.

8. People-watch on the river, where galleries, pubs, and restaurants abound.

9. Savor the sweet scents of the flowers in the fragrant garden at majestic Forsyth Park.

10. View Hilton Head Island from atop the Tybee Island Lighthouse.

flights to international destinations. Passenger airlines serving the city include Delta, American Eagle, US Airways, Atlantic Southeast, AirTran, Continental Express, US Airways Express, and United Express. This attractive airport is consistent with the style of the Historic District, so you'll feel like a Savannahian the minute you step off the airplane and enter the giant atrium that is fashioned after the downtown squares.

At the base of the escalator you'll get a firsthand preview of Southern hospitality as a member of the Savannah Area Convention and Visitors Bureau welcomes you in a newly designed Visitors' Center Kiosk filled with information about the city. As you stroll over to the baggage claim area to retrieve your luggage, glance upward for a sample of the city's beauty on a video screen that hangs overhead.

Several major car rental agencies offer vehicles at the airport, but when your getaway takes you to Savannah, you might want to leave

Park Free!

*Save yourself aggravation, change, and parking tickets by purchasing a Visitor Parking Day Pass ($5.00) from the **Parking Services Office** (100 East Bryan Street at the Bryan Street Parking Garage), the Savannah Visitors Center, or participating hotels and inns. These permits will allow you to park free for up to forty-eight hours at certain locations and are accompanied by a map of where they can be used. Among the locations at which the passes can be used are any parking meters in the Historic Downtown; any other meters with time limits of an hour or more; time-regulated parking spaces on Broughton Street; time-regulated parking spaces on River Street and its ramps; the three city-owned public parking garages (State Street Parking Garage at State and Abercorn Streets, the Robinson Parking Garage at Montgomery and York Streets, and the Bryan Street Parking Garage at Bryan and Abercorn Streets); the city-owned public parking lots on Liberty Street, Montgomery Street, and River Street; and the lot at the Savannah Visitors Center at 301 Martin Luther King Jr. Boulevard.*

the driving to others. Choose from taxis, ornately decorated horse-drawn carriages, tour-company shuttles, or hotel vans.

More than one hundred registered taxis offer transportation to and around Savannah; one-way fare from the airport to the downtown business district is $18.00 for one passenger and $5.00 for each additional passenger. (Private limousine service is also available; the fare is $15 one-way or $25 round-trip, per person.)

The city's efficient public transportation system, **Chatham Area Transit (CAT;** 912–233–5767), also offers a free shuttle service in the Historic District from downtown hotels, inns, and the Savannah Visitors Center; tickets to other Savannah locations are 75 cents. CAT buses run daily (except Thanksgiving, Christmas, and New Year's Day) from 6:00 A.M. to midnight. Should you decide to drive your own car in the downtown area, pay attention to the street direction signs (one-way streets are common) and be forewarned that the pace is mellow. Every day is Saturday in Savannah. Traffic winds slowly around the squares in the downtown grid (thanks to Oglethorpe's imaginative design), and only two four-lane roadways will get you up and over these intricate street patterns.

Opinions on the parking situation in the center of Savannah range from "plentiful" to "pitiful." Public on-street parking often seems inadequate for the volume of downtown workers and visitors, especially during festivals or at the height of the tourist seasons of spring and fall. The city's parking enforcement attendants are dutiful, and the leisurely pace of Savannah might cost you an $8.00 to $16.00 parking ticket (depending on how quickly you send your payment in) if you linger too long at mealtime, for instance. If you must park, do so in one of three city parking garages located centrally to restaurants, shopping, and hotels (see sidebar on page xvi). Most private inns also offer limited parking spaces for guests, and all major hotels offer parking garages. If you're in town only for the day, a choice central lot is **City Market Parking** (200 West Congress Street; 912–236–2949), where parking is $4.00 for unlimited hours. The garages are open Monday through Thursday from 7:00 A.M. to 7:00 P.M.; Friday from 7:00 A.M. to 1:00 A.M.; and weekends ($7.00 per day) from 7:00 A.M. to 3:00 A.M.

All that about driving and public transportation being said, *walking* is perhaps the best way to discover this city of no hills. However you arrive in town, leave the machinery aside and stroll the Historic District, at the very least, on foot. You'll hardly find a need for wheels at all, in fact, if you bring along a good pair of walking shoes.

If you choose to walk, heed these words of caution: The streets and sidewalks range from slate, brick, and cobblestone to concrete surfaces, and all have settled through the years, leaving some treacherously uneven spots. To avoid trips or falls as you explore, pay attention to the cracks and bumps that cross your path. Rubber-soled shoes are best, but even these can be slippery on wet cobblestone. Walkers should also keep their street smarts finely tuned. Savannah's slow pace and Southern hospitality give the city a small-town ambience, but it *is* a city, and street crime is not unheard of. In the evening, enjoy the nightlife on River Street or in City Market, but stay in well-lit, well-traveled areas, as tourists are prone to be fair game for purse snatchers. Review your evening itinerary with your hotel or inn concierge, take travel suggestions from locals who are familiar with the territory, and never walk Savannah's streets alone at dark.

During the Civil War General William T. Sherman spared Savannah from burning but captured the city and presented it in 1864 as a "gift" to President Lincoln ("I beg to present you as a Christmas Gift, the City of Savannah . . . "). Today Savannah can still be called a gift, but don't save her for a special occasion. Its comfortable climate is an invitation for visits every day of the year. Stroll through colorful foliage that changes seasonally, sip mocha

Helpful Hints
for Visiting Savannah

Enhance your visit by attending to certain tenets of travel. First, be courteous and tread lightly on sweet Savannah. Realize that this is a city that has only recently opened its heart to the world. Films such as Forrest Gump, Midnight in the Garden of Good and Evil, *and* The Legend of Bagger Vance *have contributed to Savannah's sudden notoriety and have lured millions of tourists to experience its charms. These Hollywood-born sirens, together with Savannah's splendid fountains, resplendent gardens, and refined historic homes, have attracted so many curious visitors that the city government recently imposed strict limits on the number of tour buses allowed through the city's squares. Amazingly, the influx of tourists has failed to erode Savannah's reputation for hospitality. All her citizens ask is that you respect their historic treasures and private spaces.*

Second, pack lightly. The lightweight attire necessary in Savannah goes from extremely casual during the day (shorts and jeans) to moderately casual in the evenings (jeans, skirts, and blazers). A semitropical climate brings seasonal mean temperatures of fifty-one degrees in winter, sixty-six degrees in spring, eighty degrees in summer, and sixty-six degrees in autumn. The city is humid, even in winter, and according to locals, there are no good hair days here.

Third, be prepared. If you come in late summer, fall, or spring, bring insect repellent to combat sand gnats—tiny biting bugs also known as "no see-ums." These pesky insects usually come out in early morning or late afternoon, or whenever the temperature hovers pleasantly at sixty-five to seventy degrees. Prepare, too, for rain showers and thunderstorms, especially common on summer afternoons.

at an outdoor cafe, and, along about 5:00 P.M., settle on the porch of an inn or snuggle on a City Market bench as the setting sun warms your cheeks. Watch the locals and listen to the night sounds. Every once in a while, remind yourself that paradise has a new Southern hostess whose grace is truly irresistible. Succumb.

FOR MORE INFORMATION

Contact the **Savannah Area Convention and Visitors Bureau,** 101 East Bay Street, Savannah, GA 31401; (912) 644–6401 or (877) SAVANNAH. Request a free Visitor's Guide or ask for the city's bed-and-breakfast reservation system. On the Internet: www.savannahvisit.com.

Most Romantic Places in Savannah

MOST ROMANTIC RESTAURANTS

The Hunter House, Tybee Island
The Sapphire Grill, Savannah
The Pink House, Savannah
The Boar's Head, Savannah

MOST ROMANTIC LODGINGS

The Magnolia Place Inn
The Hamilton-Turner Inn
The Westin Savannah Harbor Resort
The Gastonian
Granite Steps

BEST PLACES TO KISS

The top of the **Tybee Island Lighthouse**
In front of the fireplace at **The Pink House Tavern**
Standing at the water's edge on **River Street**
Sitting on the back row of the ferry to **Hutchinson Island**
In the back seat of a **private carriage tour**

Savannah's Best-Kept Secrets

George's of Tybee Island

The Savannah DeSoto Hilton

Nita's Place

Venus de Milo

The view of the city from Hutchinson Island

Most Romantic Places to Have Drinks

The riverfront, one of the few places in the country
where drinking on public streets is still allowed.

17Hundred90 Tavern

The bar at The Hunter House, Tybee Island

The City Market courtyard

Planter's Tavern (inside The Pink House)

Best Places to Watch the Sunset

River Street

The Lightship Tavern on Wilmington Island

Tybee Island's north beach

Hutchinson Island

The Harborview Room at the Savannah DeSoto Hilton

Savannah's Best Cultural Offerings

Savannah Onstage
City Lights Theatre
The Savannah College of Art and Design (SCAD) Film Festival
The Savannah Symphony Orchestra
The Savannah College of Art and Design Sidewalk Art Show

Savannah's Best Indulgent Desserts

Chef Philip Branon's bread pudding at The Boar's Head
Triple-layer chocolate cake at Café at Main
Chocolate eclair at The Six Pence Pub
Peach cobbler at Mrs. Wilkes'
White chocolate coconut cream pie at The River House

Most Romantic Festivals

First Saturdays on the River
Shakespeare in the Park
Christmas Tour of Homes
Spring Tour of Gardens
Oktoberfest on the River

Heart
of the City

Love on the Docks
SAVANNAH'S HISTORIC WATERFRONT

FROM WHITECAPS THAT ARE WILDLY TOSSED by the wind to sparkling ripples that turn golden as they dance along the river in the afternoon light, Savannah best reveals its watery roots in its historic riverfront district.

You can visit strictly for the Old World ambience of its historical architecture, but you will almost invariably be drawn toward the natural beauty apparent along the waterway that teases the city's boundaries. Breathtaking sunsets over the Savannah River, lush subtropical vegetation, and the busy charm of the shipping traffic ensure that delight is to be found in getting your feet wet in Savannah.

PRACTICAL NOTES: Be wary of spring and summer showers that bring sudden downpours. Bay and River Streets get crowded at night, and parking is limited and difficult along these narrow, busy roads. Your best bet might be to park at the Bryan Street Parking Garage and brave the cobblestone ramps or the steep stairs that lead from Bay Street to River Street down at the riverfront. You might also avoid both cobblestones and ramps by riding down to River Street on the public elevator beside City Hall, near the Hyatt on Bay Street. Also note that advance reservations are required at the Hyatt's Windows on the River.

DAY ONE: afternoon

When you arrive at the riverfront, check into the **Olde Harbour Inn** (508 East Factor's Walk; 912–234–4100 or 800–553–6533; $169 to

Romance AT A GLANCE

♦ Bask in the grandeur of the beautiful **Olde Harbor Inn** (508 East River Street; 912–234–4100) before strolling the riverfront.

♦ Relish a quiet drink at **MD's** (2 West Bay Street; 912–236–1234), a modern jazz bar overlooking the river, and dine at the **Windows on the River** (2 West Bay Street; 912–236–1234), located within the Hyatt Regency.

♦ Sample the sounds of Southern jazz, rock and roll, or bluegrass at **Bernie's River Street** (115 East River Street; 912–236–1827), one of many pubs that will satisfy your soulful taste for music.

♦ Explore the shops of **River Street** then lunch at a seafood eatery, **The Shrimp Factory** (313 East River Street; 912–236–4229), or try the eclectic **Cafe Metopole** (109 Martin Luther King Jr. Boulevard; 912–236–0110).

♦ Investigate steamship replicas at the **Ships of the Sea Maritime Museum** (41 Martin Luther King Boulevard; 912–232–1511).

♦ Ride the high seas on a riverboat as the **River Street Riverboat Company** (departing from River Street behind City Hall; 912–232–6404) shows you the sights that only sailors see as they arrive at the Savannah port.

♦ Dine at the cozy **Oyster Bar** (411 East River Street; 912–232–1565) before calling it a day.

$219), where each of the twenty-four suites overlooks the caramel-colored Savannah River. Check-in is at 3:00 P.M., but your room may be available earlier. Drop your bags and glance out the window. You'll marvel at what lies across the Savannah River, only a stone's throw away. Bursting from the water's edge, a new hotel surrounded by palm trees and elegantly polished by a dazzling pool teases your senses. Furthermore, the massive glass-front facility that lies adjacent to the hotel sparks even more conversation. This is Savannah's newest attraction—Hutchinson Island—where conventioneers gather at a resplendent trade center and enjoy the elegance of a five-star hotel. (But that's another visit for another day.)

For now, feast your eyes on the exquisite nineteenth-century furnishings of your spacious living room and one (or two) bedrooms. You have a fully equipped kitchen, but wine, cheese, and cold soft drinks are served in the inn's elegant parlor each afternoon, so don't waste any time preparing a snack. Put on your most comfortable, low-heeled, rubber-soled shoes and begin your afternoon exploring on the riverfront.

This afternoon is for staking out the territory, so hold on to your credit cards until tomorrow. River Street is a two-day affair with several surprising interruptions. For one, a stroll from almost anywhere within a 5-block radius of the river can offer even landlubbers a taste of the shipping industry as smokestacks from loaded container ships puff above the buildings along Bay Street. If you're faint of heart, stay away from the riverfront when a ship passes almost within splashing distance and its horn blasts a greeting. As the Georgia Ports Authority woos international commerce up and down the winding channel, an ordinary day on the waterfront can become an exhilarating experience in a matter of minutes.

Partake of River Street from one end to the other, but do it casually, strolling the sidewalks and browsing as if you had weeks to spend here. Forget the list of things to do. Let tiny pubs lure you in for relief from the heat or shelter from the rain with music ranging from Irish folk to bluegrass. Raise a glass to the generations of sailors who sought comfort here before you. Savor the musty scents of wood-plank floors and weathered brick before you return to the promenade of more than seventy-five galleries, boutiques, artists' studios, and restaurants. Restored with charm and taste, original cotton warehouses offering glimpses into Savannah's past house most of these businesses.

Return to the inn and relax a while at your window overlooking the river. As the sun begins to set, the sights and sounds of the riverfront take on a new aura—one that is certain to inspire picturesque photographic memories.

Freshen up for the evening ahead, then mingle with other inn guests in the parlor. If you'd rather share a quiet moment alone with your mate before dinner, stroll west down to the Hyatt Regency hotel via the bricked walkway along the riverfront, viewing the bridge and the giant freighters moored downriver at the Georgia Ports Authority terminals.

DAY ONE: evening

Once you reach the Hyatt, take the glass elevator up to **MD's** (inside the Hyatt Regency, 2 West Bay Street; 912–238–1234; inexpensive), Savannah's most comfortable and picturesque place to relax by the river. Select a table for two near the window and order cocktails. If you're lucky, a huge ship will pass in front of this third-level bar and you'll be within a few feet of sailors from remote ports who stand curiously on deck upon their arrival. As jazz plays softly in the background and a loud blast from the ship startles those below on the riverwalk, you may be tempted to applaud as the vessel passes beneath a bridge that appears to be too low to accommodate its height.

DINNER

Dinner at the Hyatt's adjoining **Windows on the River** (2 West Bay Street; 912–238–1234 or 800–233–1234; expensive) is a *must*, and reservations are suggested prior to your arrival. Try the catch of the day and ask the chef to prepare it to your own taste (grilled, blackened, sautéed, or fried). If a freighter passes by during your dinner here, you'll find yourself in a three-dimensional wonderland as mirrored walls reflect its magnificence above, behind, and all around you and your partner. Top off the evening with a Savannah favorite: warm bourbon pecan pie topped with a scoop of vanilla bean ice cream.

If you're more in the mood for light fare, head west on River Street. The late afternoon scene is like that of a shady park as rays of light warm the riverfront. You've probably exhausted your feet shopping so settle in at **W.G. Shuckers** (225 W. River Street; 912–443–0054; inexpensive). Be daring and join the late day regulars for twenty-five cent oysters (Monday through Friday, 4:00 to 7:00 P.M.).

For after-dinner entertainment **River Street** (parallel to Bay Street, one level down) rivals New Orleans's Bourbon Street. Take the public glass elevator (adjacent to the Hyatt) that glides gently down to the river level, where a lively crowd will beckon you into the colorful nightlife. You never know whom you'll meet along the rocky sidewalks. Crooning balladeers, comical magicians, a renowned flutist, or even a few street beggars blasting their trumpets for pennies may be among those River Street ramblers. You're nearly certain to meet Robert the Picture Man, a diminutive, elderly man wearing an Atlanta Braves baseball cap turned backward. This popular Savannah character has been making the rounds downtown for years, and for a mere $10, he'll shoot a Polaroid photo of you and your mate. Within a couple of minutes, he'll hand you a personal Savannah souvenir encased in a cardboard frame.

Let your mood decide where you might stop along your stroll down River Street. The riverfront is the best place to let your hair down, and a couple of rowdy nightspots may bring out the best (or worst) in you. The best Southern songwriting this side of the Mississippi beckons at **Bernie's River Street** (115 East River Street; 912–236–1827; inexpensive). If you're into down-and-dirty blues, check out the boisterous crowd at the **Bayou Cafe** (on the ramp at 14 North Abercorn Street; 912–233–6411; inexpensive). Or if you're so inclined, try a frozen specialty drink—such as Sex on the Beach, a delectable concoction of cranberry and raspberry juices with peach flavoring and vodka—at **Wet Willie's** (101 East River Street; 912–233–5650; inexpensive). Then settle down on a riverfront bench and keep an eye out for the passing freighters. The twinkling lights of port terminals and the traffic inching its way toward the towering bridge provide a dazzling backdrop. After drinking in this riverfront light show, return to the Olde Harbour Inn and snuggle into the fresh linens. Let the lapping of the river against the seawall lull you to sleep.

DAY TWO: morning

Rise early with the sun, step out onto the riverfront and watch a city built on maritime history come alive in a colorful mist. A blanket of fog as thick as meringue will hover over the glassy river, creating a ghostly coverlet. A tugboat will surrender its berth nearby to set the stage for a giant freighter that chugs along the path toward the Georgia Ports Authority. If this sight leaves you breathless, hold on to the arm of your companion and greet the cast and crew of the sailing vessels with a hearty Southern wave. After all, they are only a few feet away, almost within shouting distance.

Then gaze down the land side of this historic concourse lined with shops. River Street will glisten as downtown workers polish the streets with thick sprays of water. Joggers will dance along the long walkway that stretches from one end of the street to its boundary and just as the fog begins to vanish, a horn will blast, announcing the arrival of yet another giant ship. As a few lone gulls swoop down

Eighteenth Century Love,
Nineteenth Century Evenings

*Cimb the steep ballastone stairs that lead to Old World romance in an old cotton warehouse and watch the freighters glide along the river as two Savannahians in love woo your taste buds. Husband-and-wife team Charlene and Philip Branan purchased **The Boar's Head Grill and Tavern** (1 North Lincoln Street; 912–651–9660; moderate) a few years ago and brought the art of cooking into this rustic dining establishment with an exposed kitchen. Their dream restaurant is filled with delights, including a captivating bar that greets you upon your arrival. If there's a wait, climb aboard a bar stool and converse with the locals in this unique building that was constructed in 1780 as a warehouse for cotton brokers. Then ask for a window-front table and dine by candlelight, first sampling Philip's famous Savannah she crab soup thick with crabmeat and rich with a cream base and hint of sherry. Ask Charlene to bring two spoons so you can share a bowl to leave room for another of the chef's most popular entrees, sautéed grouper Française, with lemon caper butter sauce. Don't leave without dessert; Philip's warm chocolate bread pudding is divine.*

to retrieve remnants of yesterday's popcorn spilled onto the coblestones, this golden scene will turn to broad daylignt as you head back into the inn for some early morning refreshment. Create that perfect cup of coffee for your mate and smile. You'll have spent nothing for this splendid morning spectacular.

BREAKFAST

Delightful continental-style fare served in a charming breakfast room awaits you, so don your cushiest pair of walking shoes and reach for the credit cards as you and your mate prepare for a day of exploration and shopping. Enjoy a hot cup of coffee and homemade pastries or muffins and fruit before braving the day.

Around 10:00 A.M. head west on **River Street** past an array of colorful shops, ranging from those filled with relics of Savannah's maritime industry to intimate clothing stores brimming with the perfect attire for this city's subtropical climate. Don't miss **Regatta Sportswear**

and Gifts (15 East River Street; 912–232–7323) where souvenirs abound, as well as great sportswear for your trip. **Jonathan Arthur** (5 West River Street, on the bottom level in the Hyatt Regency; 912–447–0330) offers pricier gift items, designer clothing, and even Christmas ornaments. Farther west, check out **Land & Sea Wear** (209 West River Street; 912–232–9829) for the latest sportswear for men and women and an array of Savannah T-shirts, sweatshirts, and golf shirts. Steps away is **Nautical Ned's** (213 West River Street; 912–232–9829), another popular gift shop.

Head back east and visit **The Brass Crab** (205 East River Street; 912–233–3485), one of Savannah's oldest shops, to buy (what else?) a brass crab, ranging in price from $7.95 for smaller crabs to more than a hundred dollars for larger ones.

DAY TWO: afternoon

LUNCH

With bags filled with Savannah relics, walk east toward your room at the inn to lighten your load. Then freshen up and step back out onto the riverfront. **The Shrimp Factory** (313 East River Street; 912–236–4229; moderate) is calling! You won't miss any passing ships if you ask for a window seat, then order anything from the sea in this festive eatery. Everything here, from fried shrimp to crab stew and even freshly made shrimp or crab salad sandwiches, is spiced to perfection!

Or if you're looking for something different, cross busy Martin Luther King Jr. Boulevard and lunch at one of Savannah's most likable new eateries. The eclectic **Cafe Metropole** (109 Martin Luther King Jr. Boulevard; 912–236–0110; inexpensive; closed Wednesday) was once the home of a Greyhound bus station and still bears a likeness to its former tenant. Naked concrete floors and huge roll-up doors remain, but the delicious scent of baking bread now fills the room. Choose a table and select a light lunch—maybe a fresh spinach salad adorned with pine nuts, roasted red peppers, calamati olives, feta cheese, and homemade dressing. Enjoy the artwork that adorns the walls.

Heading east on River Street, you'll come across one of Savannah's most well-known landmarks, a tribute to those in love with their trade, their mates, and the sea. The famous *Waving Girl* statue commemorates the life of Miss Florence Martus, a vivacious, red-haired woman who began waving at passing ships during the late 1800s when she was a teenager assisting her brother in keeping a lighthouse on the island of Elba, just a short distance from Savannah. Her legendary gestures—waving a white kerchief by day and a lit lantern by night—were said by some to be signals to her lover who had been lost at sea. Others say he had sailed away, and her daily ritual—in rain or shine—was an effort to be the first to greet him upon his return. Miss Martus died in February of 1943, but this famous monument still greets vessels and their crews entering Savannah's ports.

Just a few feet from the *Waving Girl,* an unusual torch pays homage to the 1996 Summer Olympics. The copper and steel monument honors sailors from all over the world who competed in the yachting events held off the coast of Tybee Island.

Take a brisk walk down the riverfront to benches located in front of the Hyatt Regency Hotel for a full view of the ships passing beneath the **Eugene Talmadge Memorial Bridge**. As the spirit of adventure overwhelms you, clasp hands and climb the steep, rocky stairs that are parallel to the Hyatt. At the top, you'll land on Bay Street. Just a couple of blocks west is the intriguing **Ships of the Sea Maritime Museum** (41 Martin Luther King Boulevard; 912–232–1511), where you'll find intricate replicas of the sinking *Titanic* and the SS *Savannah,* the first steamship to cross the Atlantic Ocean. The museum's hours are from 10:00 A.M. to 5:00 P.M. Tuesday through Sunday, and admission is $5.00 for adults and $4.00 for students and senior citizens. The elegant maritime exhibit is set in the 1819 **William Scarbrough House,** a Regency-style home built, coincidentally, for the principal owner of the SS *Savannah.* Listed on the National Register of Historic Places, the site also houses the Historic District's largest garden, a peaceful haven where hundreds of couples have been wed and have hosted lavish receptions and parties. The museum's admission fee provides visitors access to the walled garden, which features lush vegetation, colorful seasonal blooms, and an enchanting pond filled with koi (exotic goldfish). A resplendent fountain offers soothing sounds of flowing water. Nestle on a bench and relish the solitude as you whisper, in your finest Southern drawl, sweet reasons why Scarlett O'Hara *really* wanted to go to Savannah when Atlanta was burning.

When you leave the museum and garden, walk a few blocks to the European charm of **Ex Libris** (228 Martin Luther King Jr. Boulevard; 912–238–2427; inexpensive), a Savannah College of Art and Design bookstore, gift shop, and coffee shop. Its ornate iron staircase leads to floors filled with artwork, supplies, books, and periodicals. Overstuffed couches placed throughout the building allow for comfy reading breaks as you peruse the shelves. A third-floor gallery will entice you to samples of student artwork that changes monthly.

Or maybe you want to spend part of your afternoon outdoors and on the water. If so, grab your mate's hand and hop aboard ship for a **River Street Riverboat Company** cruise (departing from the dock directly behind City Hall at 9 East River Street; 912–232–6404). The hour-long excursion ($13.95 per adult) on a replica riverboat will take you a short distance up and down the Savannah and give you both historical and present-day perspectives on this busy port. From the water, you'll gain an appreciation for the amazing shipping industry at the Georgia Ports Authority, as well as for the historic structures back on the riverfront.

When you debark, stop for a seafood snack at the **Cotton Exchange** (201 East River Street; 912–232–7088; moderate), where you can sample the restaurant's signature crab chowder and hot garlic bread. The tavern is housed in a 1799 cotton warehouse, the old wooden beams are said to be the originals that survived a great fire of 1804. The corner booths are perfect for intimate conversations, and on brisk days the wooden windows facing the river are left open for a dockside view of commercial action.

DAY TWO: evening

DINNER

Return to the inn to freshen up and change for dinner. You won't need fancy duds, but Savannah's evenings are prone to bring out the pests (mosquitoes). Wear slacks and long sleeves to protect yourself (even in summer) and trot west down River Street to **The Oyster Bar** (411 East River Street; 912–232–1565; expensive), an eatery and pub that sits right on the riverfront and offers fresh seafood in a dark, cozy atmosphere. Reservations aren't accepted here so arrive prior to sunset to be assured of a table without wait. Choose from a wide selection of imported beers and prepare to feast on hush puppies (a Southern favorite) that taste as sweet as dessert. Order the crab-stuffed flounder and leave room for dessert farther down the river.

If you're hungry for seafood, seek atmosphere, and enjoy saving money, order an appetizer here at The Oyster Bar (don't share this secret with your waiter). The grouper fingers are hearty and fresh (plenty for two) and accompanied by two house salads and drinks will give you a real Savannah meal for less than $20.

Follow your senses west to **The River House Seafood and Bakery** (125 West River Street; 912–234–1900; moderate). Aside from seafood (which you've consumed in huge quantities since your arrival in Savannah), the restaurant's specialties are its desserts. They include European pastries, white chocolate cream pie, chocolate eclairs, and more! Coffee is brewed individually to taste using French press bodums and a variety of condiments are arranged to spice up your coffee in Old World flavor. Savor this time together as you wrap up a delightful day in Savannah!

River Street has indeed taken on a new persona since your first introduction to it by morning light, and your seafaring adventures don't have to end. When you're ready to make your own waves, stroll slowly back to your lush accommodations at the Olde Harbour Inn. As Scarlett would say, "Tomorrow is another day."

FOR MORE ROMANCE

River Street shops are filled equally with unusual treasures and ubiquitous souvenirs. Just for fun, climb the stairs to **Toy Smart** (2 Lincoln Ramp; 912–651–8888). You will discover not only the secrets to many magicians' tricks but also a full range of novelty items and great games. Don't miss the color of **Savannah Sails and Rails** (423 East River Street; 912–232–7201), where kites of all sizes, shapes, and subjects hang within inches of one another throughout the old building. Another shop worth exploring is **Gallery 209** (209 East River Street; 912–236–4583), where thirty local and regional artists show their unique paintings, wood sculptures, ceramic art-work, pottery, art glass, and jewelry.

River Street is home to a variety of festivals held throughout the year. Each **First Saturday** of the month (except January and

February) features arts and crafts, continuous entertainment, street performers, and food vendors. **Saint Patrick's Day** on the waterfront is jam-packed with entertainment and color as the city turns green, and the **Savannah Seafood Festival** in May draws thousands to local restaurants vying to create the most popular seafood dish. October 3–5 is the time to celebrate **Oktoberfest** (and a decline of the summer's humidity) on the river; this annual celebration of German food and beverages provides continuous entertainment. For more information on activities along the waterfront, contact the **Savannah Waterfront Association** (912–234–0295).

Monumental Revelations

STROLLING THE STREETS OF SAVANNAH AND BEYOND

THIS SHORT JAUNT TO THE CITY is planned for art lovers seeking some quiet time. During this getaway, you'll view the city's generous art offerings and stroll through intimate historic passageways, then enjoy succulent food from the sea and be pampered in a lavish inn. Even if you're not an artist, the warm morning sun splashing rays of light through the branches of live oaks, the energy of the street awakening, and the scent of homemade pastries on the soft breeze will surely provide an inspiring backdrop for a perfect weekend of art appreciation and solitude.

PRACTICAL NOTES: Reserve a bike-taxi from **Savannah Pedicab** (912–232–7900) for your evening on the town.

DAY ONE: morning

BREAKFAST

Your escape begins first thing in the morning. Arrive in the city early while the home-baked Savannah rum cake at **The Gallery Espresso** (6 East Liberty Street; 912–233–5348; inexpensive) is still warm. At one of its outdoor tables in the heart of the Historic District, sample the cake along with a hot cup of Southern pecan coffee or a piece of fresh fruit. One of Savannah's premier coffeehouses, it's popular with locals as well as visiting movie stars like Demi Moore. Watch your step as you descend into the tiny eatery where artwork is displayed on aged brick walls that occasionally echo with the sounds of a poetry reading or live acoustic guitar music.

14

Romance
AT A GLANCE

♦ Sip coffee and dine on fresh pastries at *The Gallery Espresso* (6 East Liberty Street; 912-233-5348).

♦ Take an audio tour of the city and experience the romance of an era where elegance ruled.

♦ Share a leg of freshly cooked fried chicken and steaming old time Southern fare at **Lady & Sons** (311 West Congress Street; 912-233-2600) and walk off your calories in a breathtaking museum filled with romance.

♦ Get cozy in your lavish room at **The Ballastone Inn** (14 East Oglethorpe; 912-236-1484) before dining in an art gallery at **Bistro Savannah** (309 West Congress Street; 912-233-6266).

♦ Explore an old fort and gaze at the passing ships at Savannah's **Fort Jackson** (Highway 80 East; 912-232-3945).

After breakfast, take a walk about 6 blocks to the **Savannah Visitors Center** (301 Martin Luther King Jr. Boulevard; 800-444-2427) to rent **Tours on Tape,** a self-guided walking tour of the Historic District, narrated by a professional tour guide. For $12 you can select two tapes; for this itinerary, choose the ones called "Around the Squares" and "Nineteenth-Century Stroll." Depending on your mood, you can skip ahead, delay, or ignore any suggestions on the tape, but don't miss the birthplace of Juliette Gordon Low, the founder of the Girls Scouts; the Telfair Museum of Art; or the Owens-Thomas House.

Set out from the Visitors Center and begin your tour of some of Savannah's most notable historic sites. Your first stop may be the childhood home of one of America's best-known women. Climb the steep stone stairs of the **Juliette Gordon Low National Birthplace** (10 East Oglethorpe; 912-233-4501). This masterfully designed home, now a U.S. Girl Scout property and Savannah's first National Historic Landmark, was created by architect William Jay in 1820 in English Regency style for future Supreme Court Justice

James Moore Wayne. William Washington Gordon and his wife, Sarah, were the first of the English-born Gordon family to live in the home; William Gordon served as mayor of Savannah. The home was left to William Washington Gordon II and his wife, Eleanor Kinzie Gordon, the parents of Girl Scout founder Juliette, who spent her childhood there. Now one of Savannah's most popular tourist attractions, the home, restored in 1986, is furnished with many of the Gordon family's original items. Honeymooning couples may enjoy the painting of Niagara Falls by moonlight—a souvenir the Gordons purchased some years after their own honeymoon to that romantic spot. Among the outstanding architectural features of the house is a magnificent winding staircase that is set against a backdrop of a rose-colored glass window. The house is open from 10:00 A.M. to 4:00 P.M. daily; closed Wednesday. Admission is $6.00 for adults.

Juliette Gordon Low died in 1927 and was buried in **Laurel Grove Cemetery** (802 West Anderson Street; 912–651–6772).

DAY ONE: afternoon

LUNCH

Long about 11:30 A.M. your stomach will begin to growl; before the growl turns to a howl, head north up Bull Street to West Congress Street. Turn left onto Congress and walk west 3 blocks to City Market. Close your eyes for a second, and let the aroma of frying chicken lure you to your final destination. Lines have started to form but don't shy from this first impresssion. Hungry diners are there for only one reason—there's hardly a place in the country where you can eat like this! So claim your spot in line. The wait will be worth the pound or two you'll gain after you and your mate succumb to pure Southern cuisine—fried, mashed, creamed, and candied—at **Lady & Sons** (311 West Congress Street; 912–233–2600; moderate). Jerry Shriver of *USA Today* enjoyed his "most memorable meal of 1999" here. In his comical review he talked of "waddling" to and from the endless buffet. "If someone had reached for something on my plate, he would have lost a limb," Shriver said.

Within seconds of settling into your cozy table for two, an attractive waitress will dash over carrying a plate full of hot cheese biscuits, rolls, and fried cornbread. Beware! She may break into song at any moment, crooning favorites like "Moon River" or "Georgia on My Mind." Then, before you've even tipped her, she'll freshen your glasses with sweet tea and instruct you to head to the buffet before the line gets too long.

You'll do yourselves a favor if you don't fill up on biscuits before you see what's in store. The restaurant's owner, Paula Deen, has become world-famous for her crunchy fried chicken, black-eyed peas, mashed potatoes, turnip greens, and macaroni and cheese. For lunch or dinner, you can return to the "trough" as many times as you are able, but save room for dessert. Each day brings out favorites like peach cobbler, banana pudding, and chocolate cake. There's a menu to order from, but we recommend the buffet no matter how good the items on it sound.

Head east from the restaurant to Barnard Street, then south 2 blocks to Telfair Square. There you'll find the oldest art museum in the South. English architect and Savannahian William Jay's design creativity is most evident in the Telfair House, today part of the **Telfair Academy of Arts and Sciences** (121 Barnard Street; 912–232–1177). Built for Alexander Telfair, son of Georgia Governor Edward Telfair, in 1820, the home was left to his two sisters who had lived with him. In accordance with the will of Mary Telfair in 1875, the building was opened as the Telfair Museum of Art in 1886, after her death. It has remained a

Arts and Crafts

Choose a bench, cozy up, and enjoy the architecture surrounding **Chippewa Square,** *where Savannah's founder, General James Oglethorpe, was finally honored with a monument in 1910. The imposing bronze figure was fashioned by Daniel Chester French, the sculptor who created the statue of Abraham Lincoln for the Lincoln Memorial in Washington, D.C. Oglethorpe, for all his hard work in planning the city, never owned any land here because the Charter of the Trustees prohibited any trustee from owning property in Georgia. Luckier citizens built beautiful public buildings, churches, and private homes near this square, however. Stroll through the neighborhood, and stop for a souvenir at the Arts and Crafts Emporium of Savannah (234 Bull Street; 912–238–0003).*

museum, and its rooms, furnished with many items and artworks owned by the Telfair family, have been restored to their original appearance. Stand together in the rotunda and imagine attending the grand-opening gala in 1883 with dignitaries such as Jefferson Davis, the former president of the Confederacy.

Designed in the Neoclassical Regency style, the museum recently exhibited a remarkable group of watercolors from the Royal Library of Windsor Castle. Donated by Her Majesty Queen Elizabeth II, the fifty-two original water-colors by the British naturalist Mark Catesby (1682–1749) had never before been exhib-ited. The Savannah museum was one of only four venues to host the exhibition.

Among the museum's permanent collection of paintings, sculpture, and decorative art are several examples of American Impressionism, including major paintings by Childe Hassam, Frederick Frieseke, and Gari Melchers. Cool off from the Savannah heat as you feast on George Bellows's luscious winter landscape *Snow Capped River*, also displayed here. Some lucky cou-ples may be fortunate enough to see the love poems and other verse of the mystical poet and artist Kahlil Gibran. The fragile artwork, rendered in pencil, is only occa-sionally displayed but is the largest existing collection of Gibran's work.

Check the schedule for listings of exhibits and special events. From time to time the Savannah Symphony Chamber Orchestra and the Coastal Jazz Association host evening concerts.

Stroll east down York Street 2 blocks to Abercorn. There lies one of the most outstand-ing examples of English Regency architecture in

Finding the Bench

When you stroll through Chippewa Square in search of the bench used in Forrest Gump, *you may be surprised to discover that no such bench exists in this park. Although the whimsical film was shot in the square, the bench where Forrest sat and told his story was merely a Hollywood prop that is now exhibited at the Savannah History Museum inside the Visitors Center on Martin Luther King Jr. Boulevard. So if you ask a pass-ing tourist to shoot a picture of you and your companion seated on "the" bench, find "a" bench instead. Then wrap your arms around each other and say, "That's showbiz!"*

the country. Another of William Jay's heralded designs, the **Owens-Thomas House** (124 Abercorn Street; 912–233–9743) is a stylish residence that offers a stunning example of wealth in the 1800s. The house was built for a cotton merchant, Richard Richardson, and his wife, Frances Bolton; the Richardsons were subjected to the misfortune of losing their home to the depression of 1820, and for the next ten years it became an elegant boardinghouse. In 1825 the Revolutionary War hero the Marquis de Lafayette paid a visit to the home and, from the ornate cast-iron balcony on the home's south side, delivered his two Savannah addresses to thousands of citizens.

The site of one of the first urban slave quarters in the South is situated in the home's outbuilding, and the Carriage House courtyard graciously opens into a lush, English-inspired parterre garden. A small sitting area in the courtyard provides just the place to absorb the beauty of the manicured shrubbery and appreciate the architectural design of the rear of the house.

Hours are Monday from noon to 5:00 P.M., Tuesday through Saturday from 10:00 A.M. to 5:00 P.M., and Sunday from 2:00 to 5:00 P.M. The cost to tour the house is $8.00 for adults.

DAY ONE: late afternoon

By now, you two must be exhausted, so check into your room at the **Ballastone Inn** (14 East Oglethorpe Avenue; 912–236–1484), an 1838 mansion just a few steps west of the Juliette Gordon Low National Birthplace. The four-story inn offers plush accommodations and a garden courtyard so beautiful that you might not want to leave the premises at all. In 1998 the owner hosted a huge auction to clear the inn of antique furnishings and decor. To the delight of visitors, more than half the rooms have been completely refurbished, repainted, and redecorated, and the same treatment is planned for all as time permits. Rich colors, soft linens, terry-cloth robes, and cordial turndown service are standard offerings. Ask for the Victoria Room ($445 to $475 per night in season), delightfully accented in gold, green, and red and equipped with a gigantic king-size bed and an equally generous whirlpool tub. Have a bubble bath to soothe your weary muscles, then toast one another downstairs while you wait for your evening transportation.

A gorgeous antique bar, surrounded by plush furnishings and floral accents, is the perfect place to share a glass of wine as the afternoon shade begins to overtake the day. As you enjoy the solitude, the room will fill with guests and even a few locals and the conversations will be whisperlike in tone in spite of the incoming crowd.

DAY ONE: evening

DINNER

You have probably had quite enough of walking today, so make arrangements with **Savannah Pedicab** (912–232–7900), a free–wheeling bike-taxi that will whisk you away to your dinner for two at City Market's **Bistro Savannah** (309 West Congress Street; 912–233–6266; expensive). At this address an 1878 mercantile building has been transformed into an elegant restaurant complete with revolving works of local artists hanging on old Savannah-gray brick walls. Sit by the window in candlelight in comfortable wicker-basket chairs and watch people go by. The restaurant, although a bit pricey, is staffed by local art students, and the cuisine is fresh, healthy, and delicious. Share an appetizer of sautéed local shrimp and Tasso ham with roasted leeks and sweet Vidalia onions over creamy stone-ground grits. The house specialty, barbecued local black grouper served with creamy stone-ground peas with a pear and apple chutney ($19.95) and pecan-crusted chicken with blackberry bourbon sauce ($14.95) are just two of several outstanding entrees not to be missed. Share one of the Bistro's spectacular desserts, such as sautéed berries over vanilla bean ice cream with shortbread cookies.

As your Pedicab driver pedals through the dark streets of Savannah to return you to the Ballastone Inn, ask for a spin around Johnson Square, where the fountains dance with light and the city gleams like a vintage postcard.

DAY TWO: morning

BREAKFAST

Rise late and let the Ballastone pamper you and your companion on your last morning in Savannah. In its bright tearoom, elaborate breakfasts (and lunch by reservation) are served Southern-style. Choose an intimate table for two in the tearoom or courtyard, where freshly squeezed orange juice accompanies a variety of home-cooked breakfast items. On Saturday the inn features a full breakfast buffet with everything from mounds of fresh fruit and egg casserole to creamy grits with butter to homemade muffins and biscuits.

After checking out, venture along Highway 80 East to Savannah's **Fort Jackson** (about 3 miles outside of Savannah; 912–232–3945; $3.50 admission) and spend the afternoon together exploring the oldest standing fort in Georgia. Surrounded by a tidal moat, the fort is located on a beautiful mass of land called Salter's Island and is ideal for picnicking. Battle reenactments and a variety of special events are frequently held here. It's also a great spot for ship-gazing—those entering Savannah's port pass closely by several times a day.

FOR MORE ROMANCE

For a truly monumental weekend, stay another day and plunder through the Savannah artifacts in the **Georgia Historical Society's** Savannah headquarters (501 Whitaker Street; 912–651–2128). Admission is free, and this magnificent building is open to the public from 10:00 A.M. to 5:00 P.M. Tuesday through Saturday. Among its thousands of artifacts and other historic documents, you'll discover original letters written by General James Edward Oglethorpe to the Trustees of the Colony, old photographs of the city, and private collections of vintage photographs donated by prominent Savannah families. Bring your camera along for snapshots of your own, taken on the steps of this 1876-designed building.

Love By "The Book"

A TRIBUTE TO *MIDNIGHT*

HOT-PINK FEATHERS FROM A BOA-CLAD nightclub singer drift across the stage as a rotund woman belts out a raucous version of "Hard-Hearted Hannah" before an audience of red-faced men in drenched shirts and giggling matrons in getups from church frocks to ball gowns. The crowd is gathered for a Savannah-style celebration of the filming of *Midnight in the Garden of Good and Evil,* and it's a group typical of those folks who partied in John Berendt's book. In the sultry air of a partially restored theater, this scene is right out of a Hollywood screenplay, but it's no movie. This is Savannah, a city that not only resembles a Hollywood set but also contains all the real-life romance of the big screen. Scenes like this are everyday occurrences here.

So if you have munched on popcorn and swooned over the stars on the big screen, a trip to Savannah will bring the script alive and put *real* stars in your eyes. Savannah, it seems, has lost her virginity to a scathing best-seller. The notoriety from John Berendt's fact-based book is transforming this subdued city-by-the-sea into an international tourist attraction raging with Hollywood hormones.

If this Savannah getaway requires that the two of you take a long drive or an extended flight to the port city, read aloud to each other or tune in to the audio version of *Midnight,* narrated by the author. Most stores sell the three-hour-long tape for just under $18. Let the dialogue lure you into the world of illicit romances, voodoo discoveries, self-made wealth, and Southern social graces. If time allows, rent the video of Clint Eastwood's *Midnight* movie. The characters'

Romance AT A GLANCE

♦ Spend the night in the **Hamilton-Turner Mansion** (330 Abercorn Street; 912–233–4800), once the source of plots and subplots in tales from Midnight in the Garden of Good & Evil.

♦ Enjoy breakfast in the garden of good and evil at **Clary's Cafe** (404 Abercorn Street; 912–233–0402), where you might just spot a Midnight character.

♦ Take a Midnight walking tour with a real **Victorian Lady** (call first for a meeting place; 912–236–1886).

♦ Share a slice of gourmet pizza in the courtyard of the **Cafe at City Market** (224 West St. Julian Street; 912–236–7133) and then take your camera to the scenic graveyard that made Midnight famous.

♦ Relive the days of Johnny Mercer at **Hannah's East** (20 East Broad Street; 912–233–2225) and share a plate of barbecue at one of Savannah's oldest and most popular eating establishments, **Johnny Harris** (1651 East Victory Drive; 912–354–7810).

names have been changed and the story line differs, but you'll see many Savannah locals and a few recognizable real-life sets.

PRACTICAL NOTES: You'll hardly be impressed by a book-themed itinerary if you haven't read John Berendt's *Midnight in the Garden of Good and Evil,* so do so before coming to Savannah. Make advance reservations for the Hamilton-Turner Mansion. Hannah's East and Clary's (both popular among book-loving tourists) attract crowds daily, so guarantee yourselves seats by arriving early for meals or performances. (Neither accepts reservations.) Call Hannah's East first if you want to hear Miss Emma Kelly. Due to occasional health problems, her schedule is subject to change. Mercer House is a private residence, and the owners request that you keep your distance by viewing from the square or sidewalk. Don't venture beyond the iron gate.

DAY ONE: morning

Arrive in Savannah to the languorous melodies of the movie soundtrack. After you cross the bridge, head toward one of the book's most recently energized hostels. The **Hamilton-Turner Mansion and Gift**

Shop (330 Abercorn Street; 912–233–1833; $169 to $310) is the former home of Berendt's character Mandy, known to Savannahians as Nancy Hillis. After the book's publication Hillis attempted to make a go of the place as an inn and museum, entertaining guests with songs and tales of her escapades. But financial problems and battles with the local historical review board finally led her to sell out to a Savannah couple who have restored it to its original magnificence.

History and Mystery

"*I don't think that the book has destroyed or changed Savannah at all,*" *remarked author John Berendt. "It has only made it apparent to more people that it is a beautiful city. In Savannah, people get a little of both worlds—they may be interested in the book, but at the same time they'll get a history lesson. It's all combined. It makes for a very good experience.*" *Make your visit a combination of history and* Midnight *romance. When the clock strikes midnight, embrace on the steps of Savannah's gold-domed City Hall.*

When the mansion was owned by Hillis, a hot-pink feather boa sometimes adorned a huge carousel-horse ornament affixed to the house. It was a sign that "Mandy was in," according to Hillis. The horse is gone, but Hillis has been retained by the inn's owners as a staff member and will delight you with tunes (if you ask) and tales of *Midnight*.

Built in 1873 for Samuel Pugh Hamilton, a former banker and mayor, the Victorian-style inn, on Lafayette Square near the Cathedral of Saint John the Baptist, is furnished throughout with Empire and Renaissance Revival antiques. Fourteen exquisitely furnished suites include luxury bathrooms with Jacuzzis or restored antique Victorian claw-foot tubs. Many have working fireplaces and private balconies overlooking the square.

Now walk a few blocks away to a *Midnight* breakfast at a Savannah landmark.

BREAKFAST

Start your day like Luther Driggers, the eccentric character who threatened to contaminate Savannah's water supply with his vial of poison. Feast on *Midnight* for breakfast at **Clary's Cafe** (404 Abercorn Street; 912–233–0402; inexpensive), a lively eatery where, according to the menu, "Savannahians have been enjoying great food and lively conversation since 1903." Since the release of Berendt's best-seller in 1994, the conversation has been getting even livelier. The crowd today includes those who have dined at Clary's for years, augmented by a hearty mixture of tourists and curiosity seekers. Owners Michael and Paulette Faber bought the restaurant in 1994 shortly after the publication of *Midnight*. Since then, thousands have flocked to the diner to partake of the atmosphere, purchase book memorabilia, and scout the location for real-life characters depicted in the book. Recently, when the owners' lease ran out, the landlord considered not renewing it. But after several months of negotiating, the disputes were ironed out. Clary's is still thriving on *Midnight's* success, and the owners promise seats to all who enter this *Midnight* haven.

As you walk in the door, a glassed-in display case offers *Midnight* newsletters, Lady Chablis postcards, "the Book," and related mugs and T-shirts. On the far side of the room that once housed a pharmacy hangs a large stained-glass mural of the "Bird Girl." If possible, sit against the wall near the stained-glass window and engage in people-watching as you await your order. True to Berendt's statement that "every word is overheard," every word is *still* overheard in Clary's today, so save any tête-à-tête musings of your own for later.

Neither of you should try to count calories here. Indulge yourselves instead, with a Clary's honey pecan waffle with a side order of country ham, bacon, or sausage. Other calorie-laden Southern breakfast items not to be missed include a sinful plateful of biscuits drowning in sausage gravy.

Take your sugar high on a daylight tour of this city made famous by *Midnight*. See Savannah by "the Book" by taking a "Book Tour." Most major tour companies offer a morning and afternoon two-hour tour that takes you through downtown and out to Bonaventure Cemetery. If you don't mind crowds, the most colorful tour—and the most entertaining—is hosted by **Hospitality Tours** (135 Bull Street; 912–233–0119). Ask for tour guide Pat Tuttle, whose Southern drawl will give you a real taste of the Old South. Costs range from $15 to $18 per person, depending on the tour company you choose. Be sure to make reservations.

The Bird Girl
of Savannah

The famous "Bird Girl" statue featured on the cover of John Berendt's *Midnight in the Garden of Good and Evil* is a priceless Savannah treasure that once adorned a grave in the beautiful Bonaventure Cemetery. Owing to the influx of tourists trampling over the gravesite for photographs of the sculpture, the family had the monument removed and safely displayed at the **Telfair Academy of Arts and Sciences** (121 Barnard Street; 912–232–1177). It can be viewed from 10:00 A.M. to 5:00 P.M. Tuesday through Saturday, from 1:00 to 5:00 P.M. Sunday, and from noon to 5:00 P.M. on Monday. Admission to the museum is $6.00 for adults.

If you prefer a more intimate, personalized tour, the **Victorian Lady** (321 East Fifty-fifth Street; 912–236–1886) will tailor your tour according to "just how and what you want to see." Ardif Wood, your hostess, will flaunt a thick Southern accent and don Victorian attire; she'll even bring along an empty martini glass that you can take to Bonaventure Cemetery for a photo prop. The standard walking tour is $15 per person for a minimum of four people, $30 per person if there are only two in your group. The half-day rate is $200, and a ten-hour "Book" extravaganza tour that includes dinner is $325.

The Victorian Lady will take you (on foot) to **Monterey Square,** located on Bull Street between Taylor and Gordon Streets. Named to commemorate the Battle of Monterey during the war with Mexico, the square contains a monument honoring Casimir Pulaski, a Polish nobleman who was mortally wounded during the Siege of Savannah while fighting for the Americans. The likeness of Pulaski—who was the highest-ranking foreign officer killed in the Revolutionary War—was recently restored. During the filming of the movie *Midnight,* the statue was removed for repairs and replaced by a fake monument that served as a prop. The Hollywood statue now lies in a Warner Brothers prop lot, and Casimir Pulaski has been returned to his perch.

Mercer House is on the square's southwest corner at 429 Bull Street. With a rich history that spans more than a century, Mercer House, designed by John S. Norris and completed in 1871, is perhaps the finest example of Italianate architecture in the city. The most stunning architectural features of the house are its ornamental iron-work accents, which include cast-iron window pediments, eight balconies, and a striking sidewalk fence. A lush garden, complete with a pond and fountain, separates the main house from a handsome carriage house (both are hidden from view by a tall brick wall).

Complete restoration of the home was achieved by the late antiques dealer Jim Williams, who is credited with restoring nearly seventy Savannah homes. The modern-day fame of Berendt's work has attracted thousands of camera-clicking tourists to the home, a private residence owned by Williams's sister, and not open to the public. At press time Mercer House was being offered for sale. Several interested parties, including a few celebrities, had explored the home, but no one had purchased it.

Still in Monterey Square, you'll view the **Congregation Mickve Israel** (20 East Gordon Street; 912–233–1547), the only Gothic synagogue in America. It is the third oldest Jewish congregation in America and the first one established in the South. (See Itinerary 5.)

Book tours also take you past the offices of Sonny Seiler, Williams's defense attorney (played by Jack Thompson in the movie), at 447 Bull Street. Seiler, who still practices law there, is the proud owner of UGA, the bulldog mascot to the University of Georgia football team. Sometimes you can spot Seiler walking to nearby **Forsyth Park** (another favorite shooting location for director Eastwood).

The structure located at 450 Bull Street might look familiar to you who have seen the movie version of *Midnight*. Built in 1857 for Edmund Molyneus, a British consul and one of the most assertive men in Savannah, it also served as the home of Henry Rootes Jackson, one of the city's wealthiest men. Today the building is home to the Oglethorpe Club, an institution for old Savannah families. It played a major part in Eastwood's film as gaily dressed women (the Married Women's Club) marched up its stairs for their weekly bridge-club gathering.

When your tour ends, visit **The Book Gift Shop** (127 East Gordon Street; 912–233–3867). Owner Deborah Sullivan will direct you to *Midnight* memorabilia for your gift-giving needs— maybe a Mandy-style feather boa will tickle your loved one's fancy. Hours are 10:30 A.M. to 5:00 P.M. Monday through Saturday and from 12:30 to 4:00 P.M. Sunday, with extended hours during the summer. (Call the shop after hours for a recorded message that will deliver a true *Midnight* experience.) Book Tours leave from the shop at 9:30 A.M. and 1:00 P.M. Call ahead to arrange pickup anywhere in the Historic District.

DAY ONE: afternoon

LUNCH

Make His or Her Day

"Hospitality here is everything that Southern hospitality is rumored to be all over the world . . . When I came to Savannah last year, I saw 'the Book' displayed everywhere. I thought it was the Bible," said actor and film director Clint Eastwood. Treat your mate to some old-fashioned Southern hospitality. Purchase an autographed copy of Berendt's best-seller and present it as a gift over a romantic dinner at Elizabeth on 37th (105 East Thirty-seventh Street; 912–236–5547; moderate), one of Eastwood's favorite places to dine.

Walk a few blocks toward the river and head over to **City Market** on West St. Julian Street between Ellis and Franklin Squares. Lunch awaits at the **Cafe** at **City Market** (224 West St. Julian Street; 912–236–7133; moderate). Dine under the awning outside and try the homemade pizza with toppings of your choice on a crispy crust. The crab cakes are divine, and one of the several tasty pasta dishes is served with spicy chicken.

Plan to spend the remainder of the afternoon wandering through beautiful **Bonaventure Cemetery** (Bonaventure Road; 912–651–6843), a 160-acre graveyard along the Wilmington River. The cemetery scenes in *Midnight* brought such crowds that there is now a hefty booklet of rules and regulations for visitors, so don't plan to picnic or consume martinis on the granite bench that hosted Miss Harty and Berendt.

Instead, wander along the roadways overhung with live oaks to see the other attractions that have brought notoriety to Bonaventure: the grave of Noble Jones, a member of General James Oglethorpe's founding party; the graves of the parents of Pulitzer Prize–winning poet Conrad Aiken, who died in a murder-suicide; the grave of Aiken himself, where a bench inscribed with poetry serves as a marker; and the graves of songwriter Johnny Mercer and his wife, Ginger. Danny Hansford, Williams's lover, the violent character that died in Mercer House, is buried here too, but don't look for Williams's grave—he is buried in his hometown, Gordon, Georgia.

The story of the cemetery is another example of how Savannahians *do* like their parties. Bonaventure was once the site of an elegant plantation, and the house caught fire one evening while guests were dining. Legend claims that the guests took their dinners outside and continued to eat and drink by the light of the burning structure. Berendt's book suggests that these spooky revelers can be heard partying to this day.

As the afternoon wanes, the sun should be just right for a dusk to remember on the Wilmington River. Find a bench along the shoreline and hum k.d. lang's version of the Johnny Mercer hit "Skylark." Take your companion in your arms and watch the day slowly end. Leave Bonaventure before dark.

DAY ONE: evening

Romantic afternoons segue into sensuous evenings, so head back downtown to Bay Street and climb the dark stairs to **Hannah's East** (20 East Broad Street; 912-233-2225), where Emma Kelly, the "Lady of 6,000 Songs," plunks Johnny Mercer hits at 6:30 P.M. on Tuesday, Wednesday, and Thursday. Impress the bartender and order a Pale Rider beer—Clint Eastwood's own brew—at the place where its creator christened it, then sit close to the piano and stay a while. "Miss Emma," a Savannah legend, is a crowd pleaser and thrives on the lyrics written by Savannahian Johnny Mercer. While raising her ten children, this church-going songstress and personal friend of Mercer's drove 60 miles to Savannah from Statesboro to play and sing. Emma is so valuable to the club that a special lift was installed to assist her in getting upstairs.

DINNER

Take a cab from Hannah's to one of Jim Williams's favorite restaurants. Both Williams and Berendt graced this eatery frequently, and today **Johnny Harris** (1651 East Victory Drive; 912-354-7810; moderate) is known as "the place where Clint Eastwood ordered a barbecue special." Founded in 1924, this classic Savannah establishment was a sophisticated supper club in the 1930s and 1940s, and it still hosts ballroom dancing every Saturday night. Gentlemen should bring a jacket if they intend to get out on the floor. The atmosphere is dark and cozy, and the menu includes specialties like crabmeat au gratin and a selection of dishes with the famed Johnny Harris barbecue sauce.

If you're in the mood for a nightcap, go back to Hannah's East and listen to Ben Tucker's outstanding jazz. Afterward, ask your cab driver to take you east down tree-lined Victory Drive to ghostly Bonaventure Road. You'll pass Bonaventure Cemetery where, if you stop for a moment just outside its gates, roll your windows down, and listen carefully, you might just hear the voodoo priestess Minerva chuckling as she hobbles down the graveside road.

Back at the Hamilton-Turner Mansion, as you climb the stairs to your suite, pause and imagine the mansion full of guests, partying until dawn, as the ghost of *Midnight*'s legendary Joe Odom toasts your day in Savannah.

For More Romance

If you're still up for *Midnight* challenges, let this day stretch toward the next one at **Club One** (corner of Bay and Jefferson Streets; 912-232-0200), the home of The Lady Chablis. Tourists crowd into a smoke-filled cabaret where female impersonators perform several nights a week. Since Hollywood swept Chablis away with a six-figure salary to play herself in the screen version, she performs here only one night a month. Call for each nights' show times and performers. A schedule of events is also available online at www.clubone-online.com. When Chablis is performing expect to pay a premium (prices start at $25 per person) and catch the later show, at 10:30 P.M. when Chablis is usually the liveliest.

Something Old, Something New
ANTIQUING SAVANNAH-STYLE

ORTOISESHELL INLAID WITH BRASS, a porcelain vase bearing Chinese drawings, a full line of French antique jewelry— these treasures and more are scattered throughout the city in tiny shops, huge galleries, and antiques malls. Clasp your mate's hand, and pretend you're armed with a million dollars. Antiques shops in Savannah are filled with everything from 50-cent costume jewelry to $50,000 dining room suites, dressers, and armoires. Venture back in time through the corridors of dusty shops where there's something old—and something new for you—to be discovered around every bend. Explore the narrow stairways and troves containing everything from eighteenth- and nineteenth-century heirlooms to porcelain and glass trivets and old issues of *Life* magazine. Who knows—an old Victrola that's playing your song might be just the treasure you need.

PRACTICAL NOTES: Three days of walking the uneven streets of Savannah demand only two things: a pair of thick-soled walking shoes and some pocket change for lemonade. In summer the sun will bake your face, so wear sunscreen for protection; in fall the mornings are chilly, so dress in layers and tie your coat or sweater around your waist if the air warms up. Antiques dealers in Savannah are intriguing characters, so plan to spend time chatting with them about their wares. Make your reservations early at the Marshall House—its proximity to shops and restaurants makes it a popular stopover.

Romance AT A GLANCE

◆ Stay in a beautifully refurbished old hotel originally built in 1851. **The Marshall House** (123 East Broughton Street; 912–644–7896) has all the modern conveniences and the decor of days gone by.

◆ Share breakfast in a cheery courtyard at **Cafe M** (123 East Broughton Street; 912–644–7896).

◆ Peek into the past in an array of nostaligc antiques shops, discovering Savannah's fabulous array of hidden treasures.

◆ Feel just like family at **Mrs. Wilkes' Boarding House** (107 West Jones Street; 912–232–5997) as you and others dine around a twelve-seat table filled with bowls of hot fried chicken, mashed potatoes, and veggies cooked "Southern-style."

◆ Challenge your mate to a competitive game of darts in **O'Connell's** (108 West Congress Street; 912–231–8499), a cool, cozy Irish pub.

◆ Watch the sun set and dance under the stars as music flows thorugh the courtyard of City Market.

◆ Share a plate of Southern chicken potpie at **606 East Cafe** (319 West Congress Street; 912–233–2887), where a singer and his guitar serenade you beneath an ivy covered trellis.

◆ Share a nightcap in an old English setting at **Six Pence Pub** (245 Bull Street; 912–233–3151) or on the sidewalk where it's cool.

DAY ONE: morning

BREAKFAST

Drive down the city's once struggling Broughton Street for breakfast at **Cafe M** (123 East Broughton Street; 912–644–7896; expensive), a cheery courtyard enhanced by a glass roof and flourishing greenery, where "New South" fare is served on distinguished china and wrought-iron tables. Chef Andy Niedenthal has established a name for himself in Savannah even though the restaurant has only been open a short time. Order his uptown eggs Benedict (two poached eggs over oysters Rockefeller with tomato hollandaise sauce, roasted tomatoes, and breakfast potatoes) or try a lowcountry eggs Benedict, the same dish stuffed with crabmeat in the place of oysters. There are thick, gooey buns to select from and an outstanding selection called Irish oatmeal with a praline crust and flaming bananas. If you'd prefer lighter fare, try fresh peaches and cream, a true Southern experience.

Cafe M is conveniently located inside your hotel, **The Marshall House** (123 East Broughton Street; 912–644–7896; rooms are $119 to $200; suites are $249 to $349), so check in before embarking on your treasure hunt. The Marshall House combines the history of the city with a new look and furnishings. Built in 1851, the structure survived the Civil War and the Great Depression but fell into disrepair later. It reopened briefly in 1946, and closed again in 1957. A splendid $10.3 million restoration was completed in 1999. Staying in this extravagant dwelling with all its finery and Southern grace is a vacation in itself. The traditional architecture, with exposed brick-wall surfaces and heart-pine floors, is pleasantly combined with an eclectic mixture of traditional and colorful interior treatments.

For guests in search of the perfect bed-and-breakfast with all the luxuries of a modern-day facility, the Marshall House—with its four-poster beds and colorful homemade quilts—exceeds all standards. With the intimacy of Savannah's famous inns, there are plush terry-cloth robes in each bathroom, pedestal sinks, and claw-foot bathtubs. You and your mate can bring along a laptop to investigate Savannah attractions and events here (www.visitsavannah.com) as each room offers modem connections, remote-control color cable televisions, and two-line phones with dataports. Guests services include valet parking, member privileges at a neighborhood health club, a business center, a quaint gift shop, and twenty-four-hour concierge service. One of the city's finest hotels, it's also close to other Savannah landmarks, restaurants, and shopping.

A delightful and less expensive overnight alternative is the new **Comfort Inn & Suites** just off Bay Street (9 Indian Street; 800–221–2222; $69 per room, per night). Built in the fall of 2000, this friendly motel has one major amenity (aside from the price): The view of the Savannah River bridge from here is spectacular. Continental breakfast is free and there is an inviting pool to splash around in. To continue this itinerary from this less costly location, walk east down Bay Street to Whitaker Street and walk 2 blocks south to Broughton Street to start your day.

From the Marshall House, walk west on Broughton and you'll stumble across some charming shops filled with old and new. **Wonderful Things** (115 West Broughton Street; 912–447–0004) is filled with European antiques, fine linen, furniture reproductions, pillows, rugs, fire screens, and other decorateve accessories. An eclectic shop called **Willows** (101 West Broughton Street; 912–233–0780) is not only inviting, but filled with unusual items for your home. From antiques, kilim rugs, and kimonos, to books, candles, and throw pillows, shop owners will be pleased to ship any of your purchases home.

Buy your love a hand-embroidered set of linen napkins or pillowcases to spark the romance of your visit to Savannah.

Next, walk a half block east to Abercorn Street and go south for a totally different antiquing experience. **Capra • Capra** (319 Abercorn Street; 912–236–9004), at Lafayette Square, is housed in an 1888 building and furnished with Russian art and antiques, Neoclassical pieces, more than a hundred clocks, and several sculptures and contemporary artworks. Here you can recline on a nineteenth-century Hever Castle Lady Astor chaise longue with shapely legs and fine upholstery. This shop shines and is considered one of the most elegant in town. Plan to spend at least an hour here.

Your prelunch tour should also include a trip to **Southern Antiques and Interiors, Inc.** (28 Abercorn Street; 912–236–5080), where you'll find more than 12,000 square feet of eighteenth- and nineteenth-century furnishings that are mostly high-end pieces. If you see something you like but can't afford, ask about reproductions, which are available through special order.

LUNCH

For an old-fashioned midday meal, walk south down Abercorn to Jones and go west 2 blocks. The crowd will be lined up for a noon lunch at **Mrs. Wilkes' Boarding House** (107 West Jones Street; 912–232–5997; inexpensive). Get in line by 11:00 A.M. or you'll find yourself missing out on a meal that is, to borrow the lyrics of Johnny Mercer, "too marvelous for words."

Eating here is like taking a trip back to your grandmother's house. You'll get a warm Southern welcome from an apron-clad hostess as Mrs. Sema Wilkes, proprietor, welcomes you and about sixty other guests at a time into the dining rooms of the 1870 house. She says grace, and once the food is blessed, the rest of the Wilkes family and staff serve up about eighteen bowls and platters of Southern-cooked vegetables, fried chicken, beef stew, mashed potatoes, roast pork, and more. Just when you think the table couldn't possibly hold any more, out comes a huge plate of cornbread and hot biscuits. A bottomless pitcher of sweet tea is on the table, and lively conversation abounds with those new friends seated around the table. Don't try to make reservations; it's a first-come, first-served arrangement here. The cost for lunch is $12 per person for all you can eat. Remember to pass the food clockwise and to carry your dishes to the kitchen once you have finished (if you're able to push yourself away from the table). Mr. Wilkes will take your money (no credit cards, please; cash is preferred, but they'll take a check "if it's good").

DAY ONE: afternoon

After lunch take a leisurely stroll back toward the river. Head west (left) down Jones Street to Barnard Street. Turn right (north) and you'll pass through Pulaski, Orleans, and Telfair Squares. Keep walking north up Barnard until you reach Bay Street. Cross Bay Street and turn left. The *Savannah Morning News* building (111 West Bay Street) is a landmark to help you find **Jere's Antiques** (9 North Jefferson Street; 912–236–2815). Across Bay Street on your left, this massive warehouse is chock-full of eighteenth- and nineteenth-century antiques and lined wall-to-wall with whatever you fancy in the way of furniture. The entire front of the building houses unusual mahogany and cherry bars, complete with stools, mirrors, and huge wooden posts. Once you've perused the offerings here, step down into the wardrobe section and wander back into the depths of the warehouse, where you'll find every imaginable kind of furniture.

If you've worked up a thirst, cross Bay Street and walk 2 blocks south to **O'Connell's Pub** (108 West Congress Street; 912–231–8499; inexpensive), a rustic bar where "everybody knows your name." Look for two empty seats at the end of the weathered bar right next to the jukebox. If you're into spirits, try a cold Old Speckled Hen. Otherwise, sip a ginger ale with lime, ask the bartender for some darts, and get competitive with your mate!

Walk west a half block to Drayton Street; go 1 block north to Congress Street, and head west on Congress to **City Market,** where you can relax in the courtyard. Enjoy the smooth sounds of Bucky and Joey, two Savannahians who have made a name for themselves playing Top 40 tunes and soft rock nightly to the after-work crowds and tourists. Their laid-back style will put you in a dreamy mood, and who knows?—maybe they'll play your song.

While you're savoring the ambience of late afternoon, pop into **The Trolley Stop Gifts** (217 West St. Julian Street; 912–233–5604), where a variety of Byrd Cookies (an old Savannah favorite) are available. Purchase a box of Benne Seed Cookies and take them with you back out into the plaza area, where you can munch Savannah-style.

DAY ONE: evening

DINNER

Since the courtyard tunes are bringing back memories (and your feet are tired), hang around here for dinner. Get an outdoor table at **Malone's** grill (City Market courtyard; 912–234–3059; inexpensive) and stay a while. Live music flows throughout the charming courtyard seven days a week as late as 1:00 A.M. You're just steps from your hotel, so dance under the stars (feet permitting) until the clock strikes midnight. If you're not too tired, venture over to the **Six Pence Pub** (245 Bull Street; 912–233–3151; inexpensive) and choose from the pub's extensive line of imported beers, including Guinness, Harp, and Bass. Then head north to Bay Street, turn left and go to your room and put your weary feet straight to bed.

DAY TWO: morning

BREAKFAST

Try a freshly baked pastry from the **Express Cafe and Bakery** (39 Barnard Street; 912–233–4683), then walk over to Broughton Street to begin your second day of treasure hunting. At **Alexandra's Antique Gallery** (320 West Broughton Street; 912–233–3999), more than sixty antiques dealers sell their wares, so bring cash if you want the best deal. There's something for every budget in this mall filled with treasures, including $1.00 items. For big spenders, dealers are quick to ship items too large to pack, so don't let convenience be a consideration for purchasing fine antiques. You'll find gifts in toys, china, furniture, and dolls. Chances are you won't walk away from this one empty-handed.

From Broughton Street walk east toward Whitaker Street. Take a right onto Whitaker and proceed south 9 short blocks. Turn right onto West Jones Street and look to your immediate left for **Arthur Smith Antiques** (1 West Jones Street; 912–236–9701), one of Savannah's most popular dealers. Two floors are filled with fine furnishings. From huge Oriental rugs to ornate glassware, paintings, and eighteenth- and nineteenth-century American, English, and Continental furniture, the shop is a maze of pieces that formerly belonged to the wealthy.

DAY TWO: afternoon

LUNCH

Meatloaf and mashed potatoes may be the rib-sticking meal you need to keep your pace, so head back to the Six Pence for some good old-fashioned pub grub. This cozy, dark eatery also boasts unbelievably delicious French onion and potato soup, and it provides warmth in winter and coolness in summer. Settle down next to the front window or, if the day is nice, eat outside at a sidewalk table. Among the memorabilia adorning the interior are a replica of the *Titanic* ship's bell and handwritten proclamations that were presented to King George VI in 1937.

A half block away is beautiful Monterey Square. The afternoon is inviting, so find a bench and bask in the setting sun before heading back to the hotel to refresh yourself for the evening ahead.

You could also call **Old Town Trolley Tours of Savannah** (234 Martin Luther King Jr. Boulevard; 912–233–0083) and arrange to be picked up from your hotel for a breezy, open-air-trolley ride through the city. This tour allows on/off access, so when you get the urge to get off, hoof it through the afternoon's sunlit squares back to your hotel. Everything is in walking distance when you're in downtown Savannah!

DAY TWO: evening

DINNER

Add some whimsy to your evening and eat late. If you walk west on Congress Street, you can't miss **606 East Cafe** (319 West Congress Street; 912–233–2887; moderate). Touted as a place to dine "in a bovine setting," we won't give away this restaurant's claim to fame except to say that it is "udderly fantastic." If weather permits, ask for a seat on the "bovine patio," where a guitarist will serenade you. If you dine inside, ask for a corner booth where privacy (not to mention fun and games) is insured. Order a Savannah favorite—Dave's Salad—or try the owner's famous chicken potpie, a creamy version of an old Southern specialty filled with carrots, potatoes, onions, and chicken.

Head east down Congress Street, turn right at Whitaker, and proceed south until you reach Broughton. If you're up to an evening of funky music and dancing, stop in at **The Velvet Elvis** (127 West Congress Street; 912-236-0665; inexpensive), where groups like Audio Bridge with Elliot James and the Snakes appear. If jazz is your style, the hotel's jazz club **Chadwicks** (123 East Broughton Street; 912-234-3111; inexpensive), is the place to get romantic before taking the elevator to your room.

DAY THREE: morning

Sleep in on your last morning together, and share a pot of coffee and the newspaper in your room at the Marshall House. Then pack your things, leaving your car with the valet. Cross the street to **Gaucho** (18 East Broughton Street; 912-234-7414), one of Savannah's best-kept secrets. Treat your love to an airy cotton skirt and blouse or a pair of sterling silver earings from this charming boutique, then stroll west to Whitaker Street and head south. You'll discover a wonderful array of inviting shops like **Faith, Hope & Love** (425 Whitaker Street; 912-234-4673), where you can purchase a romantic reminder of the day.

The Market at Jones and Whitaker (401 Whitaker Street; 912-231-1006) offers beautiful dishes from France, hand-painted greeting cards, stationery, and freshly squeezed lemonade. **Walsh Mountain Ironworks** (417 Whitaker Street; 912-239-9818) will tempt you with intricately designed iron beds, light fixtures, and garden ornaments. On your way back toward Broughton, head east down York Street and enter the beautiful **RAF Gallery** (5 West York Street; 912-447-8807), filled with contemporary blown-glass art. Owners Raf and Marebeth will share their love story with you as you study the beauty of this inspiring artwork.

DAY THREE: afternoon

LUNCH

Isn't it delightful to spend a day in Savannah and never have to drive? Your morning shopping excursion on Broughton Street will leave you hungry, so return to the Marshall House and cross the street to **Typhoon Asian Cuisine** (8 East Broughton Street; 912–233–0755; moderate), a charming cafe filled with Asian delights. Lunch is served between 11:00 A.M. and 3:00 P.M. Reservations are suggested due to a popular $4.99 lunch special. Ask for a table for two on the upper level next to the windows. There you can watch Savannahians pass by and still enjoy the flowing fountain and pond inside the restaurant. Be careful: Many of this eatery's entrees are spicy, so ask before ordering if you're not into that culinary challenge.

Another alternative for lunch is one of Savannah's favorites, soups and sandwiches from the **Savannah Coffee Roasters Cafe** (7 East Congress Street; 912–232–5282; inexpensive). If the weather is damp, eat inside on comfy sofas that offer a perfect view of Johnson Square.

Enjoy the afternoon from the park bench in Wright Square before heading home laden with suitcases filled with Savannah treasures. As you drive over the Savannah bridge, glance outward toward the gold-domed city as it fades away.

FOR MORE ROMANCE

Give your feet a break. Climb aboard an **Old Town Trolley**—a colorful replica of an old-time cable car—for a colorful ninety-minute, open-air tour of the Historic District. You can get on or off at any of twelve stops along the way. Purchase a pass for the day by calling the tour company at (912) 233–0083. Trolleys run from 9:00 A.M. to 4:30 P.M. You'll be given a map when you board. Whenever an antiques store or art gallery strikes your fancy, hop off!

Divine Diversions
SAVANNAH'S SACRED ARCHITECTURE

I F SAVANNAH'S FOUNDER, General James Oglethorpe, were alive today, he'd be proud that America's first planned city still reflects his creativity. His ability to envision the hot, humid marshland of coastal Georgia as a lush habitat for settlers inspired him to persevere with a dream. That dream was realized in the construction of opulent homes, magnificent places of worship, and manicured settings laced with brilliant color and natural romance—a haven for those seeking solitude.

From the towering twin spires of the Cathedral of St. John the Baptist to the Gothic Revival style of Wesley Monumental Methodist Church, Savannah's eclectic ecclesiastical architecture has been compared to that of the finest cathedrals and synagogues of Europe. These architectural masterpieces inspired one writer to call the city a "mini Paris."

You two may experience a spiritual lift as you explore the splendor of these artfully designed houses of worship where many a couple have wed or renewed their vows.

PRACTICAL NOTES: Dress casually, keeping the weather in mind, and travel by foot without a tour guide. Churches and synagogues in Savannah are open to the public for viewing during the day, and all are located centrally in the downtown area near delightful sandwich shops and numerous park benches. All church tours are free of charge.

♦ Divine inspiration will send you on a spiritual walking tour through the city. See where the state's first religious service was held at **Christ Episcopal Church** (28 Bull Street; 912–232–8230) and share a picnic lunch in the shade of a picturesque square.

♦ Admire the beauty of an American landmark, **Congregation Mickve Israel** (20 East Gordon Street; 912–233–1547), the oldest synagogue in America, which houses the oldest Torah.

♦ Adore the beautiful walled gardens and rest in the plush surroundings of the city's most romantic suite at the **Gastonian Inn** (220 East Gordon Street; 912–232–2869).

♦ Share a plush window seat in an internationally known restaurant, **Elizabeth on 37th** (105 East Thirty-seventh Street; 912–236–5547), where you can dine late before ending the evening in the garden of the Gastonian Inn.

♦ Discover the oldest black church in America, **First African Baptist Chruch** (23 Montgomery Street; 912–233–6597).

♦ Share an intimate outdoor lunch of freshly baked bread and luscious salads from **Parker's Market** (2 Drayton Street; 912–231–1001).

♦ Bring your camera along to the **First Baptist Church of Savannah** (223 Bull Street; 912–234–2671), which was spared from Civil War destruction.

♦ Get wild at night and dine in a Moroccan haven, **Casbah Restaurant** (118 East Broughton Street; 912–234–6168).

♦ Share a nightcap in a private courtyard in one of Savannah's most romantic jazz bars, **Venus de Milo** (38 Martin Luther King Boulevard; 912–447–0991).

DAY ONE: morning

BREAKFAST

Don your best walking shorts and tennis shoes and pick up some fresh pastries and gourmet coffee at **Starbucks** (1 East Broughton Street; 912–447–6742) to jump-start this ecumenical, monumental adventure. Just a couple of blocks behind Barnard Street lies picturesque **Reynolds Square** (on Abercorn, between Bryan and Congress Streets), where in 1969 the Methodists of Georgia erected a **statue of John Wesley**, the founder of Methodism and the leader of the first known Protestant Sunday school in the United States. If the morning dew still glistens on the grass, share your alfresco breakfast on a park bench. Leave a few crumbs for the pigeons before you read the plaque honoring Wesley and set out to explore Savannah's houses of worship.

Two blocks west is **Johnson Square** (on Bull, between Bryan and Congress Streets. Toss a coin into one of the fountains here and, in the center of the square, pay homage to General Nathanael Greene, who died in 1786 and is buried there.

As you head south down Bull Street and across Broughton, you'll pass through **Wright Square,** a colorful business district where a large boulder marks the grave of Tomo-chi-chi, the Yamacraw Indian chief who welcomed General Oglethorpe to Savannah. In this square you'll enjoy a variety of architectural styles, beginning with the block-long **Federal Building** (125 Bull Street), formerly the U.S. Post Office, that was built of Georgia marble and granite in 1869. Combining French, Italian Renaissance, and Spanish elements, this "mixed-bag" post office is still in use today. (Look for this building in such films as *Midnight in the Garden of Good and Evil* and *Forces of Nature.*) Directly across from this site is the yellow-brick building of the **Chatham County Courthouse** (124 Bull Street; 912–652–7878). Visitors may venture into the foyer, but county business is in progress throughout; no formal tours are available. Its interior was splendidly renovated recently and is worth a look. The **Lutheran Church of the Ascension** (120 Bull Street; 912–232–4151), built between 1875 and 1879, boasts a striking window that tells the story of the Ascension of Jesus.

If you need camera film, **Damar Photo and Imaging** (8 East State Street; 912–236–6166), a Savannah institution, will set you up with a supply of film and process your photos the same day. For a quick pick-me-up, stop at **Joe Beans Coffee House** (21 West York Street; 912–231–1600; inexpensive), then explore an attractive group of quaint boutiques and antiques shops as you proceed farther down Bull Street.

Walk 1 block east from Bull Street to reach Abercorn, and then head down to **Wesley Monumental United Methodist Church** (429 Abercorn Street; 912–232–0191), an ornate structure that dates from 1876 and has impressive steeples that were inspired by Queen's Kirk of Amsterdam. The church, built as a monument to brothers Charles and John Wesley, is said to be the site where Charles wrote more than 6,000 hymns, including "Hark! The Herald Angels Sing!"

DAY ONE: afternoon

LUNCH

Just a block away, cross Drayton Street and head north to the **York Street Deli** (108 East York Street; 912–236–5195; inexpensive). Order two homemade shrimp salad sandwiches on whole wheat bread, a bottle of freshly brewed iced tea, and a slice of carrot cake to go.

With brown bags in hand, follow the building tops about 5 blocks north to the striking twin spires of the **Cathedral of St. John the Baptist** (223 East Harris Street; 912–233–4709). The towers lure visitors to the city from afar, and the church's interior is splendid and was recently restored. Its ornate stained-glass windows were imported from Innsbruck, Austria, and the murals were installed by Savannah artist Christopher Murphy. As the oldest Roman Catholic church in the state (originally built from 1872 to 1876 and then rebuilt in 1899), the cathedral is also the seat of the Diocese of Savannah and houses the Coat of Arms of Pope John XXIII. This site turns green each March 17th, St. Patrick's Day, when the cathedral's front steps are chockablock with paradegoers. Once you've explored the interior, share your brown-bag lunch in the warm sunshine that bakes those scenic steps most afternoons.

Continue your pilgrimage by walking 4 blocks north to Gordon Street's Monterey Square. You'll spend the remainder of the afternoon in the ornate **Congregation Mickve Israel** (20 East Gordon Street; 912–233–1547), the third oldest Jewish congregation in America and the first established in the South. This quiet, reverent place built in 1876 is the only Gothic synagogue in the country. Housing the oldest Torah in America, the museum that adjoins the synagogue holds more than 1,790 historical books and papers, including letters to the congregation from three presidents:

Washington, Jefferson, and Madison. Public tours are usually available Monday through Friday from 10:00 A.M. to noon and from 2:00 to 4:00 P.M., but it's best to call to confirm those times. Peruse the fascinating archives, then return to the modern-day world outside this beautiful sanctuary. Late afternoon is a favorite time of day for Savannahians, and as businesses close, the streets come alive with bikers, joggers, and in-line skaters.

DAY ONE: evening

Check into a room at Savannah's resplendent **Gastonian Inn** (220 East Gaston Street; 912–232–2869 or 800–322–6603; $225 and $275 for rooms and $350 for suites), a lavish, seventeen-suite inn with English antiques, beautiful walled gardens, and all the Southern hospitality one could seek in a single visit.

Built in 1868, the inn has developed an international reputation for pampering its clientele; fresh fruit and flowers are standard fare in every room. Ask for the Caracalla Suite, perhaps the most romantic accommodations in the city. With two working fireplaces, his-and-hers robes hanging next to his-and-hers marble sinks, and a massive step-up Roman Jacuzzi adorned with expensive draperies, the suite has its own private entrance and resembles a Hollywood movie set. An antique chaise longue is situated conveniently next to the tub, and a CD player with recordings of Chopin, Bach, and more is just an arm's length from an extravagant four-poster bed.

DINNER

The inn's concierge will direct you to **Elizabeth on 37th** (105 East Thirty-seventh Street; 912–236–5547; expensive), a famous Savannah dining experience where New Southern cuisine rules. When you call for reservations at this elegant mansion, ask for the front corner booth with padded window-bench seats. The cozy setting looks out onto the lush front yard tended to by the chef herself. Dine late (around 9:00 P.M.) and plan to spend at least two hours slowly sampling the luscious creations by Chef Elizabeth Terry. You'll find fresh seafood sprinkled with pecans and grits prepared with natural herbs, rich sauces, and fresh shrimp. Diced sweet Vidalia onions can be discovered in several entrees, and desserts are both artful in their presentation and delightful to experience.

After dinner, the gardens of the Gastonian are the perfect place for the two of you to settle in cushioned chairs to relax in the late-night cool breezes before retiring to the comfort of your suite.

DAY TWO: morning

BREAKFAST

Awaken and peer out your window at the sun-drenched gardens of the Gastonian, then make your way to a divine breakfast array that is full of colorful fruit, pastries, and fresh flowers. Even though the other guests are gathering around the dining room table, you and your mate opt to dine on the side porch, near the dining room. It is here that you'll be serenaded by the morning's birds and marvel at the beauty of the gardens surrounding the inn.

There's no better place to appreciate the architecture of Savannah than to study its details from the flourishing courtyard of the Gastonian. Another dining option is to savor the morning's cuisine amid a wealth of tropical plants and enjoy the quiet as you imagine that the affluent cotton merchants who first settled the city are to blame for the mixture of styles. As you sip your coffee and relish the last morsel of your breakfast, prepare to set foot on sacred soil today, once again wearing your most comfortable shoes.

With a map of the Historic District in hand, head north (by foot, of course) toward the river on Bull Street to **Christ Episcopal Church** (28 Bull Street; 912–232–4131), open 10:30 A.M. to 3:30 P.M. Wednesday and Friday. This was the first church established in the colony and is known as Georgia's Mother Church. John Wesley preached here and established the first Sunday school in 1736. Ask to see the church's famous "Revere bell," one of the rarest in the country.

After your tour, step out in the square and pause for a fresh lemonade purchased from one of the street vendors. The shade of

Johnson Square is enticing, so take this opportunity to nestle on a park bench and feed the pigeons before your next stop, a most sacred structure.

Walk west 2 blocks to Franklin Square. You'll pass through Savannah's City Market, but don't stop. Your tour today is of a religious nature; shopping is for another day.

In Decmeber 1777, the **First African Baptist Church** (23 Montgomery Street; 912–233–6597) was established and today claims the title of "The Oldest Black Church in North America." It also is where the first black Sunday school in North America was formed. The church houses the first museum in any area black church and contains archives and memorabilia dating the church to the eighteenth century. A very active congregation with an explosive choir encourages visitors to attend their Sunday services at 8:30 and 11:30 A.M.

Stay on Montgomery Street and walk a block to West Broughton. Continue on Broughton to Bull Street (4 blocks ahead) and turn south on Bull Street to **First Baptist Church of Savannah** (223 Bull Street; 912–234–2671). Chartered in 1800, this church was finally completed in 1833 and was one of only a few churches that remained open for worship during the Civil War. As a show of unity among all people, even during wartimes, the pastor there was known to preach on Sunday to Confederate soldiers and the next Sunday to Union soldiers after Savannah surrendered. It's time to take a snapshot of your loved one standing on the steps of this magnificent structure.

DAY TWO: afternoon

LUNCH

One block east is a delightful oasis set in the midst of the Historic District. **Parker's Market** (222 Drayton Street; 912–231–1001; inexpensive) is fast becoming one of Savannah's newest attractions. As you and your mate enter this unique market and deli, you'll probably wonder about its architecture. Built in the early 1900s, the expansive interior with its tall ceilings was once a grease-tainted automotive garage where Savannahians gathered for socializing and auto repair. Today, after major renovations, it's a twenty-four-hour haven for Savannah College of Art and Design students and downtown residents who are known for late-night shopping excursions. (There is even loft space for student rentals above the market.) Offering food that's more akin to a New York deli than a Southern one, at Parker's one can purchase fresh flowers for the impending picnic, the latest edition of the *New York Times*, freshly baked bread, and fruit, pasta, and seafood salads, along with your choice of beverage from the store's extensive collection of 350 wines and microbeers. A special shopping bag bearing the Parker's insignia is a must, as are extra napkins, paper plates, and plastic utensils. And don't forget the flowers!

Take your companion by the hand and lead her 2 blocks east on East State Street to Columbia Square, a shady and serene square that lends itself to intimacy. As the pigeons gather, share the goodies from your bag and then let your lunch settle before treading over to your final two hallowed stops.

After lunch, walk 2 blocks east on East State Street until you reach Greene Square. This is the home of the **Second African Baptist Church** (123 Houston Street; 912–233–6163), established in 1802. In the history books, the church stands out as the place where General Sherman read the Emancipation Proclamation to Savannah's citizens and promised the newly freed slaves forty acres and a mule. The church is open 10:00 A.M. to 2:00 P.M. Monday through Friday, 1:00 to 3:00 P.M. Sunday. This church was also the site where Martin Luther King Jr. gave excerpts of his famous "I Have a Dream" speech in the 1960s.

If you've still got some foot energy, head south (down Habersham Street, 2 blocks west from the Baptist church) to Troup Square. **The Unitarian Universalist Church** (307 East Harris Street; 912–234–0980), a Gothic revival–style 1851 structure, stands alone as a historic site. The friendly priest and his congregation delight in the fact that James Pierpont, a popular composer of hymns, served as music director there during the 1850s. He copyrighted his internationally beloved "Jingle Bells" in 1857 during his residence in Savannah.

At this point, you and your mate should commit to remain in a worshipful mood one more night at the Gastonian. Your revival in some of North America's most beautiful churches isn't over yet.

DAY TWO: evening

Call **Savannah Pedicab** (912–232–7900) and have them pick you up at the Gastonian. The fare is $10 each way for a party of two, not including tip. Since you've been angelic all day, it's time to get devilish! Dinner tonight will take you to another world.

DINNER

Ask the driver to take you to **Casbah Moroccan Restaurant** (118 East Broughton Street; 912–234–6168; moderate) where you'll be consumed with the mischievous spirit of Scarlett O'Hara and the charm of Rhett Butler. All hints that you're in Savannah will fade once you enter this exotic atmosphere. There is subtle lighting enhanced by gold and maroon ceilings and wall coverings. The music is mesmerizing and you'll more than likely be surrounded by locals who've discovered—and managed to keep secret—this treasure! Moroccan meals here come with silverware, but if you're in an exotic mood, feed your meal to your mate by hand, just like the Moroccans do. There is a variety of Moroccan wines (full-, medium-, or light-bodied), all reasonably priced, but ask your server for assistance. Order the delicious Kimrone bidawi as an appetizer. Featuring shrimp sautéed in tomatoes with onions, peppers, paprika, and other spices, it's available as an entree as well. Cornish hen mekalli is broiled and deliciously spiced with a light glaze of saffron and ginger, green olives, and preserved lemon peel. There are, of course, shish kebabs, and side dishes include vegetable couscous or saffron rice.

Dessert will consist of a light, sweet pastry and is served with cinnamon and nutmeg spiced coffee and . . . a belly dancer! This suggestive entertainer will put you in the mood for your next stop, Savannah's most intimate after-dinner gathering spot.

Your Pedicab driver will chauffeur you to **Venus de Milo** (38 Martin Luther King Boulevard; 912–447–0991; inexpensive) for a nightcap. You'll enter this tiny establishment and be drawn to plush sofas and a rustic bar where live jazz or soft rock will be playing most evenings from 9:00 P.M. to midnight. Order your favorite drink and either climb the narrow staircase to the upper deck or exit through a rear door into a small, enclosed courtyard where you can get intimate. Here you'll find flourishing ferns, wrought iron tables and chairs, and ivy-covered brick walls, original to the building. You can hide until the wee hours or simply enjoy the privacy of this setting (there are only three tables) as the music overflows outdoors.

Your divine trip to Savannah might be coming to a close, but you'll be blessed by the memories you've created.

High Cotton, High Times, High Tea
The Affluent Old South

AVANNAH'S OPULENCE CAN BE ATTRIBUTED to wealthy cotton merchants who ventured to this city seeking fortune and, as a result, displayed their affluence in the form of fine homes. Their desires brought some of the world's most masterful architects to the riverside city during the nineteenth century, and the efforts of late twentieth-century preservationists have now created from these masterpieces one of the most intriguing historical districts in the country. Grab your love by the hand and take off for a chance to touch the lavish furnishings in these treasured mansions, break for the elegant English tradition of "high tea," and dine where cotton once was king.

PRACTICAL NOTES: Savannah prides itself on authenticity, and home facades must adhere to the strict color guidelines of the **Historic Savannah Foundation** (321 East York Street; 912–233–7787); in other words, you won't find these colors in hardware store palettes. Pay special attention to the admirable way these homes have been maintained, and learn to appreciate the way time has aged (and motivated preservationists have preserved) these structures so gracefully. Reservations for high tea are recommended to avoid a wait.

♦ Sleep in **The Kehoe House** *(123 Habersham Street; 912–232–1020), where the stars have slept, and dine in elegance at* **45 South** *(20 East Broad Street; 912–233–1881), a restaurant where the lights are low and your table is secluded.*

♦ *See where General Sherman decided to spare Savannah from the ravages of the Civil War at the* **Green-Meldrim House** *(14 West Macon Street; 912–233–3845) and discover other landmarks that make Savannah's architectual heritage world-famous.*

♦ *Dine on "new South" cuisine in the former City Hotel.* **Moon River Brewing Company** *(21 West Bay Street; 912–447–0943) is touting an unusual new menu filled with fresh seafood dishes and unique micro-brewed beers.*

♦ *Stroll Savannah's lovely* **Factor's Walk** *(along Bay Street) and dash into the charming* **Gryphon Tea Room** *(337 Bull Street; 912–238–2481).*

DAY ONE: evening

Check into the **Kehoe House** (123 Habersham Street; 912–232–1020; $205 to $275), one of Savannah's showiest and most luxurious inns. Remember building sand castles on the beach as a child? When you round Columbia Square, this splendid structure will strike a chord in your heart, and you'll almost be able to feel the wet sand sifting through your fingertips as your castle grows taller.

At first glance, Kehoe House might appear to be too over-whelming to serve as a secluded romantic getaway, but be bold and enter. Built by iron magnate William Kehoe in 1892, the immense home was sold in 1930 and through the years took on varying per-sonae. From serving as a funeral home (a function that most suits its outward appearance) to capturing football great Joe Namath's fancy (he owned it briefly but left it vacant during that time), the house finally caught the eyes of Atlanta investors. Purchased and meticu-lously restored in 1993 by the Consul Court, an Atlanta manage-ment group, the inn offers fifteen rooms, all of them luxuriant settings for intimacy. So intimate are these suites, in fact, that recent guests have included celebrities Melanie Griffith, Demi Moore, and Tom Hanks (though not in the same rooms). Plush white terry-cloth robes await you, and Oriental rugs are scattered throughout the house. Rooms boast independent color schemes of bold blues, bright reds, and subdued greens. The public rooms, including the dining room, are so ornate and filled with massive antiques that you'll be tempted to sport a smoking jacket or fur stole just to fetch a cup of afternoon tea.

Georgia On Your Mind?

The South just may rise again if you immerse yourselves in the state's rituals. Feed your sweetheart a fresh peach (the state's symbol) as Ray Charles's hit "Georgia on My Mind" plays the state song softly in the background. Or, if the moon is full and shiny upon the Savannah River, ask the vocalist at the Hyatt's MD's lounge to croon that "old sweet song," and dance with your mate by candlelight.

DINNER

Before setting out for dinner, catch a breeze from your private veranda or step out into the square and listen to the splashing waters of the fountain. Then head to **45 South** (20 East Broad Street; 912–233–1881; expensive) for dinner. When you arrive, you'll find yourself near the front door of the famous Pirates' House Restaurant. The elegant 45 South is actually connected and run by the same owners as this popular tourist eatery. The difference in the two establishments is extreme. Elegant, refined, and quiet, 45 South is well suited for romance on most any evening. A tiny reception area with a working fireplace and cozy antique furnishings is perfect for getting reacquainted as you wait for your table. (Ask for one near the walls to fully experience the ambience of this lushly decorated establishment.) Entrees on the seasonally changing menu include fresh fish cooked to your preference and wild game (depending on the season) and a sumptuous wild rice. Desserts are special here and vary nightly, so save room. An extensive wine list is available. If you order appetizers, drinks or wine, entrees, and dessert, plan to spend $125 to $175 for a meal for two.

DAY TWO: morning

Awaken in your glamorous setting to a choice of cold cereal, fresh fruit, or a divine gourmet entree.

Walk over to 14 West Macon Street, the site of the **Green-Meldrim House** (912–233–3845). This John S. Norris–built home was designed and constructed in 1853 for wealthy cotton merchant Charles Green but is known infamously as being the temporary headquarters for General William T. Sherman. Sherman was offered the house by Green during his march with 60,000 troops to Savannah. It was during this period of destruction that Sherman presented Savannah as a gift to President Abraham Lincoln, in 1864. Asking that the city be spared, Sherman's telegram read, "I beg to present to you as a Christmas gift, the City of Savannah with 150 heavy guns and plenty of ammunition; and also about 25,000 bales of Cotton."

Today the home is the parish house for neighboring St. John's Episcopal Church and is acclaimed as the city's most expensive dwelling as well as the South's foremost Gothic-style house. It boasts features so appealing to the camera that you might want to bring along an extra roll of film to record the superb architectural details. Iron columns frame the entrance, and there's a wraparound tin-covered gallery. Venture inside, where American black walnut floors and marble mantels reflect fine craftsmanship. Tour hours are from 10:00 A.M. to 4:00 P.M. Tuesday, Thursday, and Friday, and 10:00 A.M. to 1:00 P.M. on Saturday. Admission is $5.00 for adults and $2.00 for students.

Don't miss a visit to the **Isaiah Davenport House and Museum** (324 East State Street; 912–236–8097). This beautiful Federal home was completed in 1820 by a Rhode Island builder who combined his knowledge of New England building techniques with architectural fashions of the day to create this gem. The house boasts fanlight doorways, cornices, plaster interiors, elongated columns and pilasters, and an unusual elliptical double stairway. Inside the home, which was saved from destruction by the Historical Savannah Foundation, are several Davenport family heirlooms.

The landmark is open from 10:00 A.M. to 4:00 P.M. Monday through Saturday and 1:00 to 4:00 P.M. Sunday. The last tour each day begins at 4:00 P.M. Tours are $7.00 for adults and $3.50 for students (ages seven to seventeen).

DAY TWO: afternoon

LUNCH

Take a break from history and proceed north up State Street all the way to Bay Street. It's lunchtime and Savannah's touting a new restaurant and brewery!

 Moon River Brewing Company (21 West Bay Street; 912–447–0943; inexpensive) is filled with atmosphere and tasty "new South" cuisine. (They call it "new South" because creative chefs have taken old Southern favorites and re-created them using fresh, healthy ingredients!)

Boasting a William Jay architectural design, the 1821 structure was once the City Hotel, providing an elegant respite for the rich and famous. The hardwood floors were created from floor joists from another part of the building and have been spruced up for their newest function. Ask Scott (one of the owners) to share some stories of the building's past as you cast your cares away on an afternoon in Savannah. Select a seat by the window so you can watch the Bay Street crowd shuffle by.

Hard-core visitors can order a frosty mug of the restaurant's specialty beer, brewed in massive kettles right before your eyes! The restaurant features six beers on tap all year long, ranging from a light, golden brew to stronger, dark stouts. You might want to try a popular brew called India Pale Ale (or IPA), a British beer that was originally brewed for the Imperial Colonies. It contains more hops and has a higher alcohol content than most beers. Recently, the restaurant added Cask Conditioned beer to its list. Flat by American standards, this unique blend is chilled to 55 degrees (most other beers are served at 40 degrees) and has an extremely smooth taste. Watch as the bartender draws your pint from a hand pump, unique to this type of brew. If you prefer, sample the restaurant's wonderful sweetened tea (with lemon, of course).

As you sip on a sample of Moon River's brews, try the Pinks VooDoo Soup, a black bean and pinto bean concoction with an intriguing blend of spices and peanuts! Order crabmeat stuffed shrimp served fresh off the grill, the Crab melt, or a River Fish Sandwich, a jumbo fillet of fried grouper with a crispy layer of bread crumbs and an awesome pepper sauce served on a Kaiser roll.

Walk off the calories and enjoy a refreshing outdoor jaunt on **Bay Street** and **Factor's Walk**. The scenic stretch along Bay Street is framed by the Savannah River in the background and overhanging moss-draped trees, ornate fountains, and manicured lawns in the foreground. The group of buildings Savannahians call Factor's Walk has so much personality that the setting has served appropriately through the years as a backdrop for national advertisers and photographers. Named for the cotton brokers (then called "factors"), this area served during the 1800s as a meeting place and center of commerce for cotton merchants. The top side contained offices of the cotton brokers, and the lower side, River Street, held warehouses. Ornate bridgeways connect the buildings along the bluff, and the ramps leading to the river are paved with ballasts used in ships. Step up to massive concrete benches and recline on these impressive works of art.

As you pass the stately redbrick building built in 1886 by William G. Preston, notably engraved THE COTTON EXCHANGE, note that this was once the spot where the world prices for cotton were set. Since closing in 1920, the **Cotton Exchange** has been merely a subject for photographers and visiting tourists; its interior is not open to the public. Before you continue your stroll, notice the magnificent winged-lion fountain in front of the building and the ornate iron fence with medallions of William Prescott, Thomas Jefferson, Joseph Addison, and other historical figures. Sip a cold lemonade from the white gazebo nearby that houses the City Exchange Bell, dating from 1802 and noted as being the oldest in Georgia. Having once hung in the original City Hall, it signaled the closing of the day for downtown merchants and served as a fire alarm when disaster struck.

All along Factor's Walk are a variety of quaint shops filled with both antiquities and tourist souvenirs. Shaded by huge live oaks and accented with hearty palms, this stretch of the city is enlivened by the antics of seagulls and tourist-friendly pigeons. Don't miss **Southern Ladies Hidden Treasures** (204 East Bay Street; 912–234–8014), a neat combination of antiques, heirloom jewelry, and Southern gifts to send back home. The owner, Rosemary Newman, is as Southern as they come, so ask for directions to somewhere if you want to hear a sample of the mellifluous native accent.

Farther east down Bay Street, you'll stumble across a unique monument, Savannah's **Vietnam Veterans Memorial**, a striking sculpture of a gun, a helmet, and boots situated on white marble. Still farther lies the **Chatham Artillery Memorial,** in tribute to the field unit that boasts the longest continuous service of any in the South. Performing duties in nearly every major conflict, including the Oconee Wars in the late 1700s, it escorted George Washington during his 1791 visit to the city. The Factor's Walk memorial was officially dedicated in 1986 during the unit's 200th anniversary.

From Factor's Walk, head west toward the gold-domed city hall. Bull Street lies directly south across Bay Street. For some really "high times," a visit to a spa is just the thing. You and your mate should call ahead to schedule a late afternoon arrival for your own private happy hour at **Vanilla** (101 Bull Street; 912-232-0040; moderate to expensive). You may want to repair your sunburned skin with a Vitamin C facial or relax and detoxify with a sea mud body wrap followed by a Swedish massage. Prices vary with your treatment, but this respite from the streets of Savannah will send you and your mate into an exhilarating mood for the evening.

High tea, the English tradition of serving specialized hot teas with attractively presented small portions of meat, salad, stewed fruit, cakes, and cookies, has made its way to the South. Daily between 5:00 and 6:00 P.M., Savannahians are donning their hats and gloves (or jeans and T-shirts in many cases) and partaking of this popular ritual with such vigor that you almost need a reservation to get in the door. **The Gryphon Tea Room** (337 Bull Street; 912-238-2481; moderate) offers the most tradition and elegance, while **The Tea Room** (7 East Broughton Street; 912-239-9690; moderate) rates higher in presentation and luscious sweets, scones, and assorted pastries.

At the Gryphon you'll experience the charm of old-time soda fountain days, as the store's original handcrafted fountain still remains (it has, however, been relocated). The building was the former A. A. Solomons & Co. drugstore, where banana splits and milk shakes were once the bill of fare. Original Tiffany-manufactured lamps still hang from the walls, and the establishment glistens with rich Honduran mahogany. A stained-glass mortar-and-pestle design on one wall reflects a pharmacy motif, and a gryphon clock and light-globe brackets are also original to the establishment. A hand-carved mahogany clock welcomes diners, and the window seats offer an unrivaled view of Madison Square and Bull Street.

The Tea Room is Broughton Street's way of celebrating the tradition with antique chairs, lace doilies, cut flowers, and newly tiled flooring. Salads are fresh, and each serving arrives on an exquisite piece of china, dotted with fresh fruit and flowers. Tea is served in giant, cloth-covered pots and is perfect with the sweets accompanying every entree. Share a pot of Earl Grey Supreme or Black Fruits tea. The dimly lit Library Room offers choice seating for an afternoon of solitude and sweet indulgences, and a corner table is the ultimate place for nestling. A crackling fire is the Tea Room's most seductive feature; the gold-rimmed china and the slow-paced Southern mannerisms of the staff add to the nostalgia.

This ends your opulent idyll in the city. With visions of fine homes and sumptuous dining etched in your memories, you'll have enough romance to carry you through the days until you return to seductive Savannah.

FOR MORE ROMANCE

Venture over to **V. & J. Duncan Antique Maps, Prints & Books** (12 East Taylor Street; 912–232–0338; 10:00 A.M. to 5:00 P.M. Monday through Saturday) and buy a piece of old Savannah. "The past makes a great present," says noted historian John Duncan, a former Charlestonian who is now a converted Savannahian. If Duncan is there, he'll mesmerize you with true-life tales of Savannah and its characters. You'll be enthralled by his charm.

Festivities Savannah-Style

Love Turns Green
A Southern St. Patrick's Day

EANT NEITHER FOR THE FAINT OF HEART nor for those seeking quiet surroundings, St. Patrick's Day in Savannah is revelry with a capital *R*. If you're seeking the honor and tradition of this jubilant occasion, you can find them in the sashes worn by the grand marshal and his court, at the Cathedral of St. John the Baptist, and among the old-timers riding in convertibles in the parade. But if it's an uninhibited, anything-goes getaway that you crave, a two-day stay in this city at St. Patrick's Day will have you acting more like a teenager loose in Florida on spring break. In short, St. Patrick's Day in Savannah is a chaotic celebration that rivals the fourth quarter of the Super Bowl or the final inning of the World Series. It's Daytona Beach without the Harleys or maybe even Mardi Gras without the masks. It's whatever you want to make it. Pick your poison prior to your visit, and don't be ashamed if you suddenly find yourself caught up in the spirit and sharing the middle of the street with a bare-chested, jewel-clad male belly dancer.

PRACTICAL NOTES: This festive itinerary is designed for upscale travelers seeking to partake of the greening of a city. Accommodations and restaurants listed here are the finest the city has to offer for this holiday, and most should be booked at least a year in advance to ensure availability. Definitely call ahead for dinner reservations at 17Hundred90 and for St. Patrick's Day breakfast at the Pirates' House. To blend in with the crowd, dress appropriately. From street-side vendors pushing carts loaded with merchandise, purchase a can of green hair spray, toss on some beads, and head out into the city for an unparalleled escape that can excite and energize you and your mate.

Romance AT A GLANCE

♦ While the city bursts in shades of green, you and your loved one will watch the festivities (and toast the holiday from your suite) in **The President's Quarters** (225 East President Street; 912–233–1600), an inn that honors the country's presidents.

♦ If you love a parade, then you'll love Savannah's **St. Patrick's Day Parade,** the third largest in the country.

♦ Dine in a restaurant that is cozy and refined, **17Hundred90 Inn and Tavern** (307 East President Street; 912–236–7122).

♦ People-watch along the riverfront, where bands will be playing, crazy revelers will be celebrating, and you and your mate will understand why the nation's second largest St. Patrick's Day celebration is right where you're sitting!

♦ Escape the madness and drive out to the islands to spend the evening strolling the beach at Tybee Island's north end. Your ears may be ringing from the volume of the celebration downtown, but the lull of the waves at your feet will settle your senses.

Be prepared to show your identification and pay a small admission fee to the riverfront if you decide to sample the restaurants, food, and three stages of round-the-clock entertainment. If you're interested in sampling a green beer, proof of age will get you an armband, which must be presented at each purchase. The fun and frolic will last the entire festival period (which is defined in the newspaper supplement you can pick up at the gate).

DAY ONE: evening

On March 16, at whatever time you can escape the drudgeries of your daily routine, check into one of Savannah's most popular inns. **The President's Quarters** (225 East President Street; 912–233–1600; $137 to $225) offers one of the best St. Patrick's Day parade-viewing sites in the city, as well as prime accommodations. Built in 1855, the inn was the first to be restored in 1986, and is a choice among Savannahians who are seeking a local overnight respite. Irish holiday packages start at $165 per night and include a St. Patrick's Evening Champagne Reception, a St. Patrick's

Day Tea (featuring the inn's signature Poor Man's Cake), party favors, a parade guide, and other special festivities to pamper you. Combine that with a Honeymoon Package ($399; includes the above plus a fruit and cheese tray, a private carriage tour of Savannah, a $50 dinner certificate at participating restaurants, a spray of red roses for the bride's pillow, champagne, Godiva chocolates, and an evening stay in one of the presidential suites) and you've got a first-class vacation.

All of the inns' suites are named for U.S. presidents who have visited Savannah; the John F. Kennedy suite ($185) is perfect for your St. Patrick's Day escapades. It faces Abercorn Street and the passing parade and has its own private balcony, a king-size bed, a separate sitting room, and jacuzzi bath. Have an intimate celebration in the exquisite sitting room decorated in century-old antiques. Wine and turndown service with cordials and chocolates are complimentary, and tea is served each afternoon in the parlor.

Far away from the crowds are reasonably priced rooms in new facilities. You'll have to drive into downtown Savannah or take a shuttle from Savannah Mall or Oglethorpe Mall to the Historic District where the Irish celebration continues, but if you're searching for serenity on a budget, check out these accommodations along the I-95 corridor (between Abercorn Street and I-16); the **Wingate Inn** (11 Gateway Boulevard East, exit 94 off I-95; 912-925-2525; from $69); **Comfort Inn & Suites** (6 Gateway Boulevard East, exit 94 off of I-95; 912-925-6666; $89;, or **Country Inn & Suites** (exit 19, I-95 and Highway 21; $89).

While you're near the outskirts of town, take your partner on a flight through time at Savannah's **Mighty 8th Air Force Heritage Museum** (Bourne Avenue, I-95 exit 18; 912-748-8888). Relive the romance of the men and women who served in the U.S. Mighty 8th Air Force in this moving tribute to war heros. There are interactive exhibits and a romantic courtyard filled with park benches, military aircraft, and all the right ingredients for a postwar-era romance! Admission is $7.50 for adults.

DINNER

A few steps east of the President's Quarters is **17Hundred90** (307 East President Street; 912-236-7122; expensive), which is part fine-dining restaurant and part full-service inn. The restaurant is on the ground floor, a brick-walled haven for those who appreciate good food and a friendly crowd.

Start with a dinner of local back-fin crab cakes, followed by the soup du jour and one of the chef's seafood or meat specialties. Afterward, retire to the lounge area that boasts two fireplaces and some of the most comfortable couches in the city. You can get an on-line preview of the inn and restaurant at www.17Hundred90.com.

Dance with the wild crowd at **The Velvet Elvis** (127 West Congress; 912–236–0665; inexpensive), where bands like "Truckadelic with Syrup" entertain. Beware! This is a place where you can really let your hair down, and the St. Patrick's Day crowd is about four or five decibels louder than normal.

DAY TWO: morning

BREAKFAST

Breakfast at the **Pirates' House** (20 East Broad Street; 912–233–5757; inexpensive) on St. Patrick's Day is almost as colorful as the parade itself. Arrive at 8:30 A.M. for a buffet of green grits, green eggs, bacon, sausage, biscuits, pastries, and an outstanding look at the color of this holiday. Your brisk walk from the inn will take you through the streets of downtown Savannah, where paradegoers have already started to gather.

When you arrive at the Pirates' House, you'll be amused to find a group of partiers hailing from Columbia, South Carolina, who call themselves the "Hat People." Wearing homemade hats adorned with everything from fresh fruit to fresh flowers, this crowd of old-timers returns annually for a St. Paddy's Day ritual that always begins at this famous Savannah landmark. Stick around after breakfast for some snapshots with these most obliging visitors, then head back over to your room at the President's Quarters and get comfortable.

One of the most pleasant aspects of staying at the President's Quarters during the St. Patrick's Day holiday is that you have no need to battle other paradegoers for a perch for the two-and-a-half-hour parade—your balcony is the perfect spot for watching. Even closer to the action, the staff at the inn offers a courtyard filled with an active grill and frosty libations like mugs of Guinness Stout (or hot coffee and chocolate if there's a nip in the air). You'll be the envy of those who aren't so lucky, so enjoy the second largest St. Patrick's Day Parade in the country from this comfy viewing point.

When it began in 1813, the parade consisted of a small group of Hibernian Society celebrants who marched to the Independent Presbyterian Church to honor the anniversary of the death of Patrick—a missionary said to have introduced Christianity to Ireland. The public was invited in 1824, and through the years the parade grew in size as military units, school bands, and political dignitaries—including Harry Truman and Jimmy Carter—attended. The parade-viewing stands, located in front of the cathedral, have hosted at least three other U.S. presidents: William Howard Taft, Herbert Hoover, and Franklin D. Roosevelt. Today sexy parade queens ride atop professionally designed floats, and along with other local Irish societies there are bands, Clydesdale horses, precision military units—in all, more than 200 entries to entertain you for hours.

Make "the luck of the Irish" your own. Patronize the many street vendors with purchases of a green garter, green hosiery, and a four-leaf clover for your special day on the town.

Make Your Own Luck

Once the parade ends, the revelry intensifies. Leave the privacy of your suite and walk toward the riverfront to the east of the Hyatt Regency. Peer over the wrought-iron fence from **Bay Street** looking onto **River Street**. Then step onto the Visitors Center elevator and treat yourself to Irish food and fun all along the riverfront. If you're still in the Irish spirit, from River Street climb the ballastone staircase to the west of the Hyatt and cross Bay Street. Walk a half block west to Barnard Street, and you'll find yourself in **City Market,** where the crowd is quite a bit smaller and generally more well behaved. Rock 'n' roll music will flow for hours, and you and your companion should indulge in Irish antics without restraint, for you'll have to wait an entire year to have this much fun again.

Savannahians know what they need after a hearty day of celebrating Irish-style: peace and quiet. Drive your mate to Bay Street and head for the beach by following Highway 80 east. A near-dark stroll along the North End of Tybee Island is the prefect way to slow your body down from the day's green-splattered antics.

FOR MORE ROMANCE

Come to Savannah early in the month and enjoy the serious side of the holiday with festive ceremonies leading up to St. Patrick's Day. The **Celtic Cross Ceremony and Mass,** held a week before St. Patrick's Day, starts at 11:30 A.M. at the Cathedral of St. John the Baptist. After Mass a wreath-laying ceremony is held in Emmet Park. The ceremony is both colorful and dignified. For more information call the St. Patrick's Day Parade Committee office at (912) 233–4808.

For a little more action, sit among the live oaks and enjoy grilled food and heavy foot action as the **St. Patrick's Day Rugby Tournament** brings in more than fifty teams from all across the country for two full days of competition. The second largest rugby tournament in the nation, it is sponsored by the Savannah Shamrock Rugby Club. For more information call (912) 234–5999.

Fireworks on the Riverfront
A Southern Fourth

I F St. Patrick's Day is too potent for you, then the Fourth of July on Tybee Island and in Savannah is the perfect answer to your quest for excitement and beauty in a tamer fashion. A three-day waterfront festival attracts vendors and entertainment of all sorts. Some years live symphonic music is synchronized with the exploding fireworks; other years you'll see a serene and stately Tall Ship Festival, like the one held in 1998. Whatever the year, Savannah on the Fourth of July explodes with romance.

PRACTICAL NOTES: Prepare for a saunalike experience on the streets of Savannah and the beaches of Tybee Island. The heat, coupled with the humidity of the South's most hospitable city, will leave you soaked to the skin, even after you've showered. Make your reservations at the 17th Street Inn on Tybee Island and the Hyatt Regency Savannah early and pack plenty of red, white, and blue. Savannahians like to show their colors. At the Hyatt, ask for a fourth-floor riverfront room ($25 extra); you'll be at eye level with the passing freighters. Note that the check-in and check-out times at these hotels can be flexible, but they must be arranged prior to your visit.

DAY ONE (JULY 3): afternoon

Savannah's Independence Day spirit spills over the city limits, right out to Tybee Island and a good ways beyond. Start your Fourth of July partying on the beaches of Tybee, then swing back to the city for an explosive ending to the holiday.

Romance AT A GLANCE

♦ Head to Tybee Island where the locals will put on a holday celebration by the seashore and the **Ocean Plaza Beach Resort** *(Fifteenth Street and oceanfront; 912–786–7664) will open its breezy doors to you and your mate.*

♦ *Feast while wearing your flip-flops at* **Spanky's Beachside** *(1605 Strand, Tybee Island; 912–786–5520) and then marvel at the explosive sky as fireworks illuminate the Atlantic Ocean.*

♦ *Dine in a world-famous* **Breakfast Club** *(1500 Butler Avenue; 912–786–5984) where you'll eat fluffy omelettes, crispy bacon, and creamy grits, then drive into Savannah where the fireworks will begin.*

♦ *Stay right on the riverfront at the* **Hyatt Regency Savannah** *(2 West Bay Street; 912–238–1234) where the action below is in full view.*

♦ *Bring your cameras along to record a Fourth of July celebration fit for a king in a glorious setting of old and new.*

On the afternoon of the third of July, make an early getaway to the island. Victory Drive (U.S. 80) is the perfect road to take for this celebration of independence. For a taste of Tybee Island, check into one of its oldest beach houses. The **17th Street Inn** (12 Seventeenth Street; 912–786–0602; $75 to $135) is reminiscent of Tybee's family-owned beach houses of the 1920s. There are no phones in the rooms, so climb into the antique iron bed and nap to your heart's content with no interruptions! Suites offer full kitchens, and the inn is located a half block from the ocean. If this inn is booked, the nostalgic **Lighthouse Inn** (16 Meddin Drive, Tybee Island; 912–786–0901; $75 to $135) is an option. The inn boasts a grand piano (to be shared by its musical guests) in the parlor where the beautiful Tybee Lighthouse is in full view through the picture windows. Each room offers old-time soaking tubs with claw feet, and a continental breakfast is served each morning. An expansive porch filled with wicker chairs and rockers is the perfect place to sip coffee or while the day away with a good book.

Slide on your flip-flops and stroll or drive south on Butler Avenue to the new Tybee Island Pier and Pavilion. The aroma of barbecued ribs will thicken the air, and the crowd of beachgoers will be particularly festive today. Pay the small admission fee to allow you onto the pier, where live music will take you away to the sounds of the 1950s. Shagging to the simple rhythms is one of the most popular ways to beat the heat and ring in the holiday. As fishermen reel in their catches down on the pier, stay in the cool shade of the covered dome and sip lemonade as barefoot dancers indulge in the shag, the dance of the South. Don't be bashful if you feel like dancing yourselves. Watch the simple footwork of this easy two-step and try it out shamelessly. If you falter, someone in the crowd is bound to pitch in with an impromptu dance lesson. If not, you'll have fun just trying to get it right.

DAY ONE: evening

DINNER

Catch your breath and put your flip-flops back on, then mosey on over to **Spanky's Beachside** (1605 Strand, Tybee Island; 912–786–5520; inexpensive), a popular eatery where the yellow-and-white awning means only one thing—the best chicken fingers in the world! (Former owner Ansley Williams claims to have been the first to invent the chicken finger when he discovered a use for scrap pieces of white meat. So far, no one has disputed him.) Located just steps from the Pavilion, Spanky's will be roaring on the Fourth. Sit near the window and watch the surf roll in as the crowd on the beach swells.

After you share a plate of chicken fingers and whatever else triggers your appetites, make your way out onto the pier. Along about dark, settle down in the nearby wooden swing and thrill to the explosions and color of an old-time fireworks production that makes Tybee Islanders proud. The road into Savannah will be heavily congested once the show is over—all the more reason to stay on Tybee and crawl into bed. Let the sounds of the surf sing you both to sleep.

DAY TWO (JULY 4): morning

BREAKFAST

You're just a few steps away from **The Breakfast Club** (1500 Butler Avenue, Tybee Island; 912–786–5984; inexpensive). The name speaks the truth. For years beachgoers have flocked to this tiny

Doin' the Shag

Bend your knees. Swirl. Pivot. Slide and spin. "The Shag" is the South's most romantic dance, and it is just a lesson away in Savannah. Savannahians have been relaxing their shoulders and falling in love with this popular dance since its origin in the 1950s. South Carolinians have designated it as the official state dance, and residents and visitors to the South all agree that the Shag is as much a part of Southern tradition as grits, fried chicken, and the ever-popular slang for all of you—"y'all."

So where and how does one learn the art of shagging? Contact the Savannah Shag Club at (912) 692-6229. The club meets monthly at the Holiday Inn Midtown (7100 Abercorn Street; 912-351-7100).

eatery for some of the best breakfast fixin's on the East Coast. Owner Jodee Sadowsky, a Northerner by birth, has such a renowned reputation that he was asked to cater the wedding of the late John F. Kennedy Jr. and Carolyn Bessette at Cumberland Island. Try his light, fluffy omelettes, cooked to perfection, or his buttery waffles. There's an endless pot of coffee, as well as great conversation. Be forewarned: If you eat a huge breakfast here, plan to skip lunch—that is, until late afternoon when you get to the riverfront festivities in Savannah. Food is everywhere!

For now, sprawl out in the warm sunshine of the Tybee Island strand and lounge for the next few hours on the beach. If you overhear the radios of other beachgoers, you may catch announcements about riverfront activity back in Savannah. Excitement for the evening ahead should send you to your room in early afternoon to pack and take the scenic drive down Highway 80 into Savannah.

DAY TWO: afternoon

When you reach the city, check into the beautiful **Hyatt Regency Savannah** (2 West Bay Street; 912-238-1234; $169 to $219), a luxurious place to spend a holiday evening. When you pass the mirrored foyer, you'll enter a tropical-like atrium filled with lush foliage. Romantic piano music flows as visitors mingle and glassed elevators whisk guests to their suites. Unpack and enjoy the spectacular views of the Savannah River and the huge vessels that cruise past your windows. Below the hotel, on River Street and Bay Street, crowds will be gathering early to stake out a place for watching the 9:30 P.M. pyrotechnics. When you have settled your gear and freshened up for the evening, join the masses down on the riverfront.

The Savannah Waterfront Association is cracking down on the rowdier forms of Fourth of July revelry, so you can expect entertainment suitable for all ages. The Savannah Symphony may be playing patriotic tunes beneath a starlit sky, or a brass band may be prompting young and old to shag in **Rousakis Plaza,** the covered stage area at the center of the riverfront activity. Food vendors will be out in full force. For a few dollars, you can feed your love crawfish or share a candied apple or a shrimp kabob. The prefireworks activities generally begin around 5:00 P.M., so you'll have a few hours to enjoy the music and the people-watching.

Light Up the Sky

While the crowds vie for every available viewing space along River Street for the Independence Day fireworks display, treasure your own private celebration from the opposite side of the river. Drive over the Eugene Talmadge Bridge on the Fourth of July and park along what was once a racetrack. Climb atop the car hood and wait for the lights of Savannah's downtown skyline to flicker on at sunset. Then, as the sparks fly overhead and the thousands of spectators across the water marvel at the artistry, watch the sky's colorful illumination cast a special glow on you and your mate.

DAY TWO: evening

DINNER

After you've made appetizers of the River Street fare, climb the stairs to **Tubby's Tank House** (115 East River Street; 912-354-5903; inexpensive to moderate), where you can order entrees (the grouper fingers will add spice to your evening, and the shrimp salad is fresh and crispy) or just snack some more until the wee hours. Ask for a table on the shaded outdoor deck. With an unobstructed view of the Savannah River and the lights of hovering boaters twinkling like a blinking Christmas tree, it's the ideal place for getting mischievous and sharing sweet nothings. Get ready for the sparks to fly! When the barge starts making its way to the center of the river, you'll know that the fireworks extravaganza is about to begin.

When the show is over, leave Tubby's and walk over to City Market at Jefferson and St. Julian Streets, where the **Red, White, and Blues Festival** is probably in full swing. The sounds of Dixieland bands may inspire you to dance in the streets till after midnight. When the music stops, continue your walk back to the Hyatt for a restful night in a modern, spacious suite. Your fireworks are just beginning.

For more romance

Contact the **River Street Riverboat Company** (912-232-6404) for a Fourth of July schedule of paddleboat cruises on the *Savannah River Queen* or the *Georgia River Queen.* Each offers romantic dinner cruises before and after the fireworks display, and the view of the festivities from the water looking toward land is filled with twinkling lights, color, and music.

Savannah Haunts
A Ghostly All Hallows'—or Any—Eve

I T DOESN'T HAVE TO BE HALLOWEEN for you to get spooked in Savannah. The ghosts of this city don't look too kindly on strangers and others who have invaded their territory, transformed their homes into choice restaurants, and turned their cellars into storage rooms for fine wines. Their ways of constantly reminding earthlings of their presence have led to strange sightings and outrageous sounds, creating a mecca for ghost hunters and thrill seekers. You and your companion will want to stay close during visits to Savannah's creepy quarters.

DAY ONE: morning

BREAKFAST

Never go ghost-hunting on an empty stomach! Start this hauntingly romantic day with a fresh, hot bagel from **The Bagel Place** (2 West Broughton Street; 912–233–2624; inexpensive). Then muster up your courage for some prerequisite paranormal research.

You must be a believer in the spirits of Savannah in order to experience the ghostly thrills that abound here. **E. Shaver Fine Booksellers** (326 Bull Street; 912–234–7257) is the place to research your adventure into the world of strange Southern encounters. This is a bookstore like no other in the city, a place where one could spend hours perusing hundreds of books in an old Savannah atmosphere. Located on a corner beneath shady live oaks, this store is the perfect place to

♦ *Begin your adventures at **E. Shaver Fine Booksellers** (326 Bull Street; 912–234–7257), a quaint bookstore where Savannahians have been gathering for conversation and intellectual reading material for years.*

♦ *Stay in a true haunted house at **17Hundred90 Inn and Tavern** (307 East President Street; 912–236–7122), where the staff will haunt you with tales of strange happenings.*

♦ *Take a walking ghost tour through the streets of Savannah that will keep your companion shoulder-to-shoulder during your stay.*

get cozy with your mate. There are twelve rooms of books and each nook has its own character and style. One might enjoy a hardbound book on gardening in the airy hallway that separates an addition from the original building, and then peek around the corner to discover a wealth of paperbacks ranging in subject matter. If you're looking for books on Savannah, the store has the most complete collection of new, historical, and cookbooks around. Ask for the owner, Esther Shaver, a delightful Savannahian who will welcome you to the city and fill you in on its happenings. Pick up a copy of *Savannah Spectres and Other Strange Tales* (Donning Company; $9.95) by Margaret Wayt DeBolt, a trusted Savannahian who has personally interviewed those who have encountered ghosts. Curl up together to read these tantalizing tales beneath a live oak in **Monterey Square,** the central location for viewing the famed **Mercer House** (429 Bull Street), an 1860 mansion where a fatal shooting spawned a best-seller and a movie. Although Mercer House is not open for public tours, its beauty and mystique can be enjoyed from street level. Nearby, the former headquarters of the Savannah Art Association, located at the corner of Bull and Gorden Streets, is also the site of a tragic event that has been linked to the supernatural—a late mistress of the house once rushed out of her bedroom, lost her footing, and fell down the narrow stairs to her death. Some say she can still be seen on the staircase.

DAY ONE: afternoon

When you've finished reading ghost stories, check into the **17Hundred90 Inn** (307 East President Street; 912–236–7122; $100 to $225) for your first scare. The inn is said to be constructed on a foundation that may at one time have held another inn. Today's structure also houses an inviting restaurant, and the Federal-style buildings not only are enticing but add a sense of eeriness to your dining experience.

LUNCH

Enjoy a glass of iced tea, a cup of crab stew, and a shrimp salad sandwich in the 17Hundred90 dining room, and ask the waiter to share some of the restaurant's grisly tales. Chris Jurgensen, a German who once owned the restaurant, is said to have sensed a girl described as a heartbroken soul named Anna, who was so distraught that her lover was going off to sea that she threw herself from a third-floor balcony into the courtyard to her death. Perhaps it is her footsteps that are heard to this day, even when the restaurant is empty (especially on Sunday, when the restaurant is closed). Anna has possibly been responsible for the continuous rocking of chairs, a cold chill passing through the room on a warm day, the creaking of floorboards, and the mysterious ringing of a telephone heard from what was once her room.

Another presence, said to be of a large, aggressive female cook from the 1850s, is perhaps the result of her practice of voodoo. Regardless of the reasons for her ghostly appearance, the woman has been sighted by both employees and guests.

Just a short distance from the inn lies a street famous for its energetic spirits. At **426 East St. Julian Street** stands an attractive Cape Cod–style cottage. Shipbuilder Henry F. Willink is said to have been the first resident of this charming home, which was moved here from another location. According to author DeBolt's recounting of the tale, Willink and his young wife were aboard a ship that he was building when she accidentally fell overboard and was swept to her death by the Savannah River currents. Willink, who tried unsuccessfully to save her, grew so distraught over her death that he reportedly had trouble sleeping and would often storm out of his house to climb aboard the ship and work. One evening an apparition of his wife appeared on the boat, and when he became startled and took a step backward, he too fell. Willink was saved and eventually owned his own shipyard near Savannah, but the slamming of the front door is still said to be heard by those who have lived in the cottage.

Just down the street from the cottage is the **Hampton Lillibridge House** (507 East St. Julian Street), the site of perhaps Savannah's most infamous tale of horror. What makes the structure fascinating is that its former owner, the late Jim Williams, grew tired of the violent activities incited by the home's resident ghosts and hired the Right Reverend Albert Rhett Stewart of the Episcopal Diocese of Georgia to perform an exorcism to rid the house of its evil spirits.

Named for its builder, Hampton Lillibridge, the home is more than 200 years old and stands as an unlikely facade in a city where most other homes of its era were built of stone and brick. The home has both a widow's walk and a gambrel roof, and its beachy look often makes it seem out of place in downtown Savannah. Williams purchased the house in 1963 and had it moved to its present location from a site 4 blocks away. The house was paired with another one for the move, and the other home fell on a worker and killed him. (That house bears tales of its own; when it was a boardinghouse, a sailor reportedly killed himself by hanging from a brass headboard in an upstairs bedroom.)

The Hampton Lillibridge House had hardly been situated on its new foundation when workers began reporting strange sounds, including footsteps. Women's screams, rattling chains, and strange bumping sounds were also reported. Once, according to DeBolt's book, one of Williams's friends who went upstairs to investigate the strange

Trick or Treat

Feed your love freshly made chocolate treats from **River Street Sweets** (13 East River Street; 912–234–4608) or **Savannah's Candy Kitchen** (225 East River Street; 912–233–8411). These two sweets factories are filled with not only the finest chocolates but also homemade Savannah pralines. Peer through the window or venture inside to watch the candymakers at work, and sample a praline before you make your selection. Chocolate-covered pralines, caramel pralines, pralines with white chocolate, pralines with dark chocolate, and much, much more are here to tantalize your tastebuds.

sounds was found lying face down on the floor. He said he felt like he had just walked into a pool of cold water. Even following the exorcism, other strange happenings were recorded in the home, which was later purchased by a physician. The house is plainly marked PRIVATE RESIDENCE, so be discreet about your fascination.

DAY ONE: evening

DINNER

Another spirit-filled restaurant is the **Pirates' House** (20 East Broad Street; 912–233–5757; moderate), one of Savannah's most popular tourist attractions. This wood-planked tavern, built in 1734, is rife with the tales of the sort of seafaring men found in Robert Louis Stevenson's *Treasure Island*. It is said that Captain Flint died here and with his last breath shouted, "Darby, bring aft the rum," and that his spirit still remains in what is known as the "Captain's Room." Strange sounds and flickering lights have been reported here for years, especially in the part of the building where seamen stayed. No employee, in fact, will venture up to the top floor alone.

The convenient location to the river made the house a perfect rendezvous for pirates. Secret passageways said to lie beneath the structure served as links to the river for smugglers. One of those passageways can be viewed from the main dining room, where a massive buffet spread beckons diners every day. A mechanical pirate stands at the top of the stone stairway where the top pirates once stood.

The Pirates' House is a great place to eat while acquiring the jitters at the same time. Their menu is traditional Savannah, with favorites like red rice and shrimp Creole. Desserts are mostly made from ice cream but come every way from flaming to drenched in meringue. Coordinate your dining time with evening tour departures.

The best way to be spooked is to hook up with a professional ghost-tour guide, and Savannah boasts plenty of them. Tours last approximately ninety minutes, and continuous hand-holding with your partner is guaranteed. Take your pick. The **Lowcountry Ghost Walking Tour** (912–238–9255; $13.00 for adults and $6.50 for children ages six to fourteen) leaves from the center of Johnson Square at 5:30, 7:30, and 9:30 P.M. nightly. Departing from the

The Real Ghostbuster

*The word about town is that the most haunted house in Savannah happens to be one that the late Jim Williams owned. While you're browsing **E. Shaver Fine Booksellers** (328 Bull Street; 912-234-7257), ask for a copy of Savannah's Jim Williams & His Southern Houses ($39.95). In this coffee-table book self-published in 1999 by Williams's sister, Dr. Dorothy Williams Kingery, you'll find the frightening story of the Hampton Lillibridge house as told by Williams (in his own descriptive prose). This great restorer of Savannah's fine homes saved nearly seventy structures in the city. The frightening encounters with ghosts during the restoration of the Hampton Lillibridge home is worth the price of the book to spook you and your mate for the day's hauntings.*

John Wesley Monument in Reynolds Square is **Ghost Talk, Ghost Walk** (912-233-3896), which costs $10 for adults. **The Savannah Walks** (912-238-9255) offers a Low Country Ghost Tour that leaves shadowy Reynolds Square. Advance reservations are required for all tours 5:30, 7:30, and 9:30 P.M. nightly, which range in price from $13 to $25 per person. **Carriage Tours of Savannah** (912-236-6756) offers horse-drawn ghost tours, which may be more suitable if you've spent the day on your feet. The tour costs $17 for adults (in a shared carriage). Private tours are $65 Sunday through Thursday nights and $85 Friday and Saturday nights.

Head back to your inn after your tour to listen for the meanderings of the supernatural. Maybe you'll even share a nightcap with Anna, the 17Hundred90 Inn's lovelorn apparition. Just don't forget to latch your door.

Tomorrow, depart while it's still daylight.

FOR MORE ROMANCE

A more lighthearted look at Savannah's spirits (mingled with a little nightlife) can be enjoyed by taking a haunted pub tour with **The Savannah Walks** (123 East Congress Street; 912-238-9255). This whimsical pilgrimage to local pubs departs Monday through Saturday at 7:00 P.M., gathers at Johnson Square, and lasts approximately two and a half hours. As you visit Savannah's rustic taverns and pubs, a narrator shares tales of pirates, parties, and Prohibition. If you want to see the watering holes and tune in to folklore too, try this jaunt. The tour is $13 per person and is offered only to adults twenty-one or older.

If you're too scared to walk, take **Ghosts and Gravestones** (912–233–0083) a creepy trolley that will take you on a spirited tour near some of Savannah's most famous homes. Your guide will share some real skeletons from the closets of Savannah's finest. You'll stop in at the old City Hotel (currently the home of Moon River Brewing Company) on Bay Street and visit Colonial Cemetery, where Georgia's most influential former residents (and their ghosts) now rest. This one will keep your lover close by! Tours are $25 per person; tours pick up at **Trolley Car Gifts** in City Market; **The Hyatt Regency** Hotel on Bay Street; the Bay Street **Days Inn,** and at the company's car barn, 234 Martin Luther King Boulevard, at 7:15 P.M.

Holiday Magic
CHRISTMAS IN SAVANNAH

S AVANNAH'S WEALTH AND BEAUTY are never better displayed than at Christmastime. With thousands of twinkling lights decorating River Street, a huge shining Christmas tree in Forsyth Park, and city squares adorned with fresh evergreens and red bows, Savannah is a scene come alive from an old-time Victorian Christmas card. The ground won't be covered by snow, but love will be in the air as the Yule log is lit and the holiday season in Savannah sparks festive fireworks.

PRACTICAL NOTES: Plan to take this itinerary on the second weekend in December so that it coincides with the Colonial festivities at Wormsloe State Historic Park. Bring layered clothing just in case there's a chill in the air. Since it's been known to reach the seventies during December, you can leave your woolens at home; sweatshirts or long-sleeved sweaters are perfect for the chilly morning and can be shed later during the day. Mornings and evenings are crisp and cool, but middays can often feel springlike. Hotel and restaurant reservations for the holiday season should be made well in advance.

DAY ONE: morning

Let the Spirit of Christmas encourage you to start your journey to Savannah early in the day. From the soft colors of a Southern morning to the glittering tones of a city draped in lights at night, Savannah sparkles all day at holiday time.

BREAKFAST

 Start this crisp morning with homemade pastries, fresh fruit, and a hot cup of coffee from the **Savannah Coffee**

Romance AT A GLANCE

♦ Ring in the spirit of the season at the **Savannah Coffee Roasters Cafe** (7 East Congress Street; 912–232–5282) and stroll the city's gaily decorated squares.

♦ Check into the Christmas wonderland at the **East Bay Inn** (2 East Bay Street; 912–238–1225) where the lights will be twinkling on upon your arrival.

♦ Take the staircase through the quaint parlor of the inn to **Skyler's Restaurant** (225 East Bay Street; 912–232–3955), where crab cakes and fresh flounder will get you ready for the season in Savannah.

♦ Delight your holiday senses with a boys' choir, massive live oaks, an old Southern plantation, and a burning Yule log at **Wormsloe State Historic Park** (7601 Skidaway Road; 912–353–3023).

♦ Ice-skate to Bing Crosby's "White Christmas" beneath a ceiling of twinkling lights in a magical setting surrounded by creatively decorated Christmas trees at the **Savannah Civic Center** (Liberty and Montgomery Streets; 912–651–6556).

♦ Warm up with a cup of soup at **Savannah's Tony Roma's** (7 East Bay Street; 912–341–7427).

Roasters Cafe (7 East Congress Street; 912–232–5282; inexpensive). With cups in hand, stroll over to **Johnson Square** (Bull Street, between Bay and Congress Streets) to catch the early morning light filtering through the live oaks. From the center of the square (named for Robert Johnson, the governor of South Carolina who helped the Georgia colony), glance around at the town bedecked in holiday garb. Straight ahead is gold-domed **City Hall** dressed in fresh greenery. The lanterns of the city squares are draped in red. **The Coastal Bank** (27 Bull Street; 912–235–4400) building is adorned with giant wreaths, and the lobby of the **SunTrust Bank** (33 Bull Street; 912–944–1000) building is alive with moving dolls, twinkling lights, and an animated Victorian scene.

In leisurely fashion make your way 1 block north to Bay Street and head east toward the **East Bay Inn** (225 East Bay Street; 912–238–1225 or 800–500–1225; $119 to $199), where an enchanting stay awaits you. The lobby decor is outstanding, with newly cut garlands, a live tree, and a wealth of antique ornaments and furnishings; the setting is perfect for a Christmas-card photo. Your luxurious, brick-walled room features a queen-size four-poster bed, a generous seating area, nightly turndown service, and coffeemaker. Some rooms overlook Bay Street; ask for one of these and enjoy the views of holiday decorations at the riverfront.

Room at the Inn

Twinkling lights, candlelit lanterns, and fresh greenery are among the festive decorations of the **Historic Inns of Savannah Annual Holiday Tour** (800–379–0638) sponsored by Savannah's innkeepers in early December. Fifteen inns are open for self-guided visits from 1:30 to 4:30 P.M. on the Saturday of the tour and from 1:30 to 4:30 P.M. and 6:00 to 8:00 P.M. on the following Sunday. Tickets good for both days ($15 per person currently but subject to change yearly) can be purchased at any participating inn. Along with some holiday refreshments and the stories behind these hostelries and their furnishings, pick up some decorating ideas to feather your own holiday love nest.

DAY ONE: afternoon

LUNCH

One of Savannah's finest restaurants is housed in the same building as the inn. Take the elevator or descend the stairs to **Skyler's Restaurant** (225 East Bay Street; 912–232–3955; moderate), a dark, cozy setting where crab cakes, flounder, and lemongrass chicken dishes are prepared fresh and presented promptly. Request the table for two beneath the window at the far corner of the room. You'll be near a giant fireplace and away from the crowd of business diners and tourists.

After lunch, drive out to "Colonial Christmas" at **Wormsloe State Historic Park** (7601 Skidaway Road; 912–353–3023) to a celebration of Christmas that depicts a tradition dating from the late 1700s—the burning of the Yule log. From Skyler's Restaurant on Bay Street, turn right and proceed south down Price Street to Victory Drive. Turn left on Victory Drive and drive about a mile until you reach Skidaway Road. Turn right onto Skidaway and go about 8 miles. You'll cross narrow bridges over marshland, and when you reach the part of Skidaway that is shaded by live oaks, you'll know you're nearing this beautiful plantation.

The only plantation in Savannah, Wormsloe was settled by Noble Jones, one of the state's first colonists. In 1974 it was given to the Georgia Heritage Trust; today it features a visitor center with exhibits and audiovisual programs centering on Georgia's founding and colonial period. It is also the site of the ruins of a fortification and the Fort Wimberly earthworks.

The history of the plantation is intriguing. After Noble Jones's death in 1838, his only surviving son, George, fled the mosquito-infested lowland of Georgia with his family for a newly built mansion in Newport, Rhode Island. George retained possession of the plantation but he tired of sharing his family name with another Savannahian, so he changed it to George Wymberley Jones DeRenne. Jones's descendants still retain more than sixty-five acres of the estate. The family's white clapboard house is not open to the public, but the drive down the "Avenue of Oaks" has long served as a romantic setting for films and for lovers of all ages. A stone archway signals the entrance of the plantation, and beyond it lies a masterpiece: a narrow street shaded with huge moss-covered trees. Follow it past the Jones's home to a parking lot. Stroll through the quaint museum that boasts many personal items relating to the history of the Jones family and life in colonial Georgia. Then spend the afternoon in the beauty of the shaded ruins. A trail leads to the Skidaway River and a breathtaking view of the expansive marshes, where you'll spy wild egrets in their natural setting.

The holiday event at Wormsloe is

Just for Laughs

Get giggly with an old-time Savannah thirst quencher that'll pull no punches. The Shrimp Factory (313 East River Street; 912–236–4229; inexpensive to moderate) and River House Seafood and Bakery (125 West River Street; 912–234–1900; moderate) feature menus that tout Chatham Artillery Punch, a seasonal favorite. (The Chatham Artillery is the oldest military organization of record in Georgia.) The concoction includes wine, rum, gin, brandy, whisky, tea, brown sugar, orange juice, lemon juice— and champagne. Call a cab after consuming this holiday libation.

"Jingle All the Way"

When you glide amid the colorfully clad skaters in the Savannah Civic Center's ice rink, clasp hands and warm your hearts with thoughts of Savannahian James Lord Pierpont, composer of one of America's most beloved songs about winter.

Young James Pierpont, a native of Massachusetts, ran away to sea in 1836 and later went west to the Gold Rush with the Forty-Niners. By Christmas 1852 he was back in Savannah as the organist of the Unitarian Church, where his brother John Jr. was pastor. There he penned "Jingle Bells," originally titled "One-Horse Open Sleigh" when it was copyrighted in 1857. Pierpont also conducted a singing school, gave music lessons on the organ, and operated a retail business with his brother William. He died in Winter Haven, Florida, in 1893 and is buried in Laurel Grove Cemetery in Savannah.

In 1985 a marker honoring Pierpont was unveiled in Troup Square in front of the church, now the Second Baptist Center, where he was the organist when "Jingle Bells" was copyrighted.

held the second Sunday in December at 5:00 P.M., and admission is $2.50 for adults. While the Yule log burns, carolers, accompanied by musicians on zither and flute, will serenade you. Nibble on holiday baked goods and sip cupfuls of hot cider as you learn the strategies of colonial games and circle dances evoking the ambience of a simpler era.

DAY ONE: evening

Return to the city at twilight and watch the lights come on. The **Savannah Civic Center** (Liberty and Montgomery Streets; 912–651–6556) is transformed into a winter wonderland each holiday season with more than seventy-five decorated trees encircling an ice-skating rink. The event, created through the efforts of individual designers and businesses, benefits Parent and Child Development Services, a nonprofit agency. Admission to the "Festival of Trees" is free; if you wish to skate, the $8.00 fee includes skates. Share a steaming cup of hot chocolate from the civic center refreshment stand before walking to a casual dinner that is truly Savannah.

DINNER

Try a cup of warm baked potato soup or a flame-grilled specialty at **Savannah's Tony Roma's** (7 East Bay Street; 912–341–7427; inexpensive). It's easy to get cozy in this restaurant located in a historic landmark building. Ask the general manager to share stories of this famous structure with you and your mate.

After dinner, take a stroll to Savannah's **City Market** aglow with holiday spirit. At Christmastime the market is chock-full of unique holiday displays and unusual gifts. Spend some time searching for treats and treasures for everyone on your list—and don't forget to choose something wonderful for yourselves. Then it's back to the inn. Maybe you'll want to exchange those special gifts now.

FOR MORE ROMANCE

If you can't make it to Savannah on the second weekend in December, try for the first Friday. That's when City Market businesses host a **Christmas Open House** (912–232–4903; free) from 6:00 to 9:00 P.M. A candlelit luminaria path leads from the market's courtyard to the charming shops of this district, and owners serve complimentary hot apple cider and other refreshments as visitors peruse their holiday wares. Outdoors, strolling carolers serenade the shoppers while Father Christmas greets children.

Away from It All

Bare Feet and Fresh Oysters

A Taste of Tybee Island

THE WATERWAYS THAT MEANDER through the South Carolina Low Country to south Georgia empty into the choppy Atlantic Ocean along the shoreline of tiny Tybee Island. With its rustic beachfront business district dotted with salty bars and its scenic north beach flanked by a towering lighthouse and old-time cottages, Tybee Island is a haven for lovers seeking pure, absolute, unadulterated serenity.

PRACTICAL NOTES: Tybee Island is such a simple destination that getting here takes little effort beyond arranging for a rental car or driving your own. Pack your belongings for a long weekend in one small backpack. All you need are a pair of flip-flops, a couple of T-shirts, and a pair of jeans. Be prepared to do little, because at Tybee Island, there is little to do. If it rains during your stay, read the *Tybee News* aloud to each other. If it's sunny, walk or bike around the 2.5-mile-long island, sit beneath the shade of the pavilion on the wooden pier, or relax in the sun on the sandy beach. Make reservations at the Ocean Plaza well in advance of your visit—vacancies at this popular resort are hard to come by.

DAY ONE: afternoon

In early afternoon leave midtown Savannah by car and take Victory Drive (U.S. 80), sometimes called Tybee Road, to the east. Tybee

Romance
AT A GLANCE

♦ Drive along the scenic Highway 80 east and observe the wildlife lining the road as the gold and green marshland surrounds you.

♦ Stop for a frozen daiquiri at the William's Seafood/**Tiki Hut** right on the water (8010 Highway 80 East; 912–897–2219).

♦ Stay on the oceanfront and capture the sounds of the Atlantic's fury along this stretch of coast. The **Ocean Plaza Beach Resort** (Fifteenth Street and oceanfront; 912–786–7664) is the perfect place to stay within the sea's cool spray.

♦ Dine in a "Sea World" atmosphere where you can almost touch the tropical fish as they surround you. **The Dolphin Reef** (inside the Ocean Plaza Beach Resort; 912–786–7664) will refresh you for a Tybee Island night.

♦ Dance on the rooftop at **Fannies on the Beach** (1613 Strand, Tybee Island; 912–786–6109) and call it a day at **Doc's Bar** (10 Sixteenth Street; 912–786–5506), where a "Tybee original" will sing your favorite tunes.

♦ After breakfast among the dolphins, spend the morning listening to the sounds of the waves crashing against the rocks at **Fort Pulaski** (U.S. 80 East on Cockspur Island; 912–786–5787).

♦ Have lunch at an upscale eatery right on the beach. **The Grille** (404 Butler Avenue; 912–786–4745) is a cheery place to eat and observe the antics of seagulls right beside the ocean.

♦ Watch the dolphins jump to and fro on **Captain Mike's Dolphin Tours** (Lazaretto Creek; 912–786–5848) as the sun sets, then continue your nature excursion as you track loggerhead turtles to their nests.

♦ Dine in a tiny eatery that's salty with age, dimly lit, and cozy. **George's** (1105 East Highway 80; 912–786–9730) is one of Tybee's most treasured restaurants.

♦ Welcome the sunrise at **The Sunrise Restaurant** (1511 Butler Avenue; 912–786–5917) and scour the beach for marine life.

Island lies about 18 miles from downtown, on the Atlantic Ocean.

Along the way you'll have a glorious view of the salt marsh creeks and boaters meandering up and down the green and gold maze of marshland, and you'll discover why people love living on these islands surrounding Savannah. Tiny brown rabbits hover beneath the marsh grass that frames the highway. Skinny egrets, with their long, pointed beaks seem like thin French models on a Paris runway as they stand gracefully in the salt mudflats searching for food. Grandfathers stand along the roadside with their grand-children, dangling cane poles and crab nets.

Continue your drive east toward the ocean and about a mile after you pass a stoplight at Quarterman Drive, turn left into the whimsical **Tiki Hut** (adjacent to Williams Seafood, 8010 Highway 80 East; 912–897–2219; inexpensive), right at the water's edge.

As you park, you'll spot the colorful umbrellas and tables near the water and immediately be drawn to the thatched roof hut where locals and tourists are conversing and sipping frozen concoctions and a variety of beer and wine. The ocean breezes will be blowing in off the water, creating a heavenly start for your vacation. If some of these customers appear a little rough, it's just because they've proba-bly come in from a long day at sea, fishing or boating, and have tied their boats right up to the dock next to the Tiki Hut. Order a snack from the hut's simple menu—steamed shrimp or Low Country boil (shrimp, onions, corn, and sausage)—or try some boiled peanuts. If you can draw yourself away from this delightful oasis, get back in your car and continue your drive east toward Tybee Island.

When you arrive on the island, you'll notice that this small community of about 4,000 full-time islanders has an ample supply of colorful local characters. Affectionately called "beach bums," these inhabitants add enchantment to almost any outing. The Beach Bum Festival and parade in the spring pays homage to those char-acters, but even when you meet them in stores and at beachside eateries, they'll share island lore with you (whether you want to hear it or not).

Along with these "bums" you'll find aristocratic Savannahians who venture here for weekend retreats at family-owned beach houses and transplanted Northerners who, after traveling south for a touch of warm air, ripped off their coats and ties and stayed. Along with these regulars are day-tripping Savannahians who arrive in droves on weekend mornings and make the trek along the snaky Old Tybee Road back to Savannah in the afternoon. If you arrive a stranger on Tybee Island, you'll most certainly leave with a list of new friends from all walks of life.

You two have no heirloom house in which to hide away for a few nights here, but that's not the style on Tybee. Check into the **Ocean Plaza Beach Resort** (Oceanfront at Fifteenth Street; 912–786–7664 or 800–215–6370; $65 to $235 per night), a clean, family-owned motel—and a welcome alternative to old, rustic lodgings. Standard rooms are oversize, and oceanfront suites with kitchenettes are available. Two pools and a poolside juice bar add to the air of a Caribbean resort; if you close your eyes, you can imagine you're in the tropics.

Check into your room, then take a stroll on the pier just a couple of blocks away. Opened in 1996 in time for the summer Olympics, the $2.5 million structure was built on nearly the same site as the former Tybrisa pier, famed for its Big Band concerts from the 1940s until it burned down in the 1960s. The new pier's pavilion, the large wooden platform you'll reach before the pier itself stretches out over the water, is still a good place to hear a free concert. If no musicians are on deck while you're here, you might rent a fishing pole or two and join the anglers at the end of the pier. If you prefer to keep the fine catch you've found in each other, simply enjoy the view, then head back to your room and change (into a fresh T-shirt) for dinner.

DAY ONE: evening

Tybee nightlife is nothing else but good old laid-back fun—from miniature golf to bingo, from country-western dance lessons to bar-hopping. You two fishing buddies may want to do what lots of the locals do, beginning with swapping tales about the ones that got away. Do it over dinner, as the islanders do.

DINNER

You won't have to venture far to dine in a tropical paradise, thanks to a local who turned a lifelong dream into an upscale restaurant overlooking the Atlantic Ocean. Touted as being the place for "great food and great fun," the **Dolphin Reef** (Ocean Plaza Beach Resort, oceanfront at Fifteenth Street; 912–786–8400; expensive) is probably the most colorful and refreshing place you'll dine on your trip. A live aquarium and hand-painted murals enhance this whimsical bistro that offers fresh seafood and steaks.

Start your evening out in the lounge, where live entertainment is offered nightly. Then head to the dining room and watch the waves roll in. Take your time sampling the grilled, fried, or steamed seafood, savoring every mouthful as you watch the ebb and flow of the tide.

Stroll out onto the beach where, just in front of the hotel, comfortable chairs await. After you've rested under the stars, that second wind kicks in and it's time to hit the streets of Tybee Island's "strip," and dance the night away

Follow the brightly colored lights to the miniature amusement park located adjacent to the Ocean Plaza. The Ferris wheel ($1.50 per person) is high enough to afford a view of the ocean when the operator stops the wheel to let riders on.

Spend another dollar on a freshly made candied apple to share with the apple of your eye.

Tybee Island's Sixteenth Street is rockin' and all you have to do is walk a few steps south of your hotel, past the pier, and you'll hear the music coming from **Fannies on the Beach** (1613 Strand; 912-786-6109; inexpensive). Owner Jenny Orr opened this fast-food restaurant/bar/nightclub in 1992 and today, it's all that and more. What makes Fannies so much fun is the mix of clientele you see when you enter. There are retirees slurping on milk shakes, teenagers gulping corn dogs and chicken fingers, tourists relaxing on the deck that overlooks the ocean, and lovers dancing cheek-to-cheek to the music of a live band. Dance until your feet are numb, and then walk a half block north to Sixteenth Street, turn left, and you'll discover one of Tybee's best-kept secrets.

Chu's Secret

Comb the racks of sexy swimsuits at Tybee Island's *T. S. Chu's* (6 Tybrisa Street; 912-786-4561), the original gift shop started more than thirty stores ago by a Chinese immigrant who spoke no English when he arrived in this country. The successful entrepreneur's name has become well known to Savannahians, and his Tybee Island store is located just feet from the beautiful pier and pavilion. Select a suit that flatters your form, then indulge your sweet tooth to celebrate your new look. Share an ice-cream cone from a beachside vendor as you take a barefooted stroll together down the wooden pier that extends over the Atlantic Ocean.

Doc's Bar (10 Tybrisa Street; 912-786-5506) is the place to stop for a nightcap before walking back to your room. Charlie Sherrill (a

Jimmy Buffet wannabe) or Randy "Hat Man" Smith will be entertaining islanders and visitors alike in this seaside pub just steps from the ocean. The native dance, the Shag, will more than likely be in progress, and if you want to learn, just ask a Tybee islander at Doc's. It's an easy two-step that will bring you close together and make you feel like true Southerners. When the lights at Doc's fade, take the sandy route back to the Ocean Plaza from the beach directly in front of the bar. The moon will light your way, and the sea breeze will guide you.

DAY TWO: morning

It's difficult to sleep when the chugging of shrimp boats awakens the gulls, so jump out of bed, put on your worst pair of yard shoes, and head for the beach. Tybee Island shines in the early morning light, and if it's low tide the beach will be perfect for hunting for shells, collecting shark's teeth, or just being together. Steer a course northward using the towering lighthouse as a landmark. At North Beach, the view is clear all the way to Hilton Head. Pause to soak up the beauty, then turn around and retrace your trek southward. The aroma of breakfasts cooking will provide the incentive you'll need to tear yourselves away from the seascape.

BREAKFAST

By the light of the rising sun, share memories of the wonderful evening you had last night as breakfast is served at the Dolphin Reef restaurant. Share an omelette or try the South's favorite breakfast entree, scrambled eggs and creamy grits. Drink plenty of fresh orange juice, because the beach beckons!

There will be plenty to do later in the day, but for now, plant your bathing-suit-clad bodies in an umbrella-shaded lounge chair and spend the rest of the morning relaxing and enjoying the shoreline sounds.

DAY TWO: afternoon

LUNCH

There's something about the beach that makes you hungry, so change out of your bathing suits, put on a pair of comfortable walking shoes (or drive if you'd rather not walk about a quarter of a mile) and follow the sidewalk north on Butler Avenue to **The Grille** (404 Butler Avenue; 912-786-4745; moderate). This is a cheery place to unwind in the cool ocean breeze or, if it's too warm, in a dining room filled with greenery and ceiling fans. The patio is the perfect place to smell the salt air while dining on freshly grilled mahi (a Savannah favorite) and a cool salad.

Afterward, drive west (toward Savannah) to **Fort Pulaski** (U.S. 80 East; 912-786-5787; $2.00 per person) on Cockspur Island for an afternoon of playing among the ruins of a nineteenth-century fort surrounded by the sea. This national monument—the most impressive of Savannah's historic military installations—was begun in 1829 and completed in 1847, with Robert E. Lee as one of its original engineers. The majestic structure sits at the mouth of the Savannah River, a location that offers one of the best opportunities for capturing on film the city as well as its photogenic surroundings. The fort's weathered-brick archways are multicolored with age, and they themselves provide a striking background for souvenir photos.

A two-and-a-half acre parade ground forms the center of the five-sided fort, which has walls 7.5 feet thick. During the Civil War, Union forces used experimental rifled cannons, firing from Tybee Island more than a mile away. Much to the chagrin of the fort's engineers, the rifled artillery overcame the masonry fortification—an achievement that precipitated a global rethinking of military defense forts. Learn the whole story in the fort's visitor center.

Outside the fort's moat, where the marshland meets the ocean, are 537 of the most picturesque acres in the state. A tiny lighthouse beckons shrimpers into nearby small marinas, and waves crash onto the rocks surrounding the fort. Also to be found here are picnic areas and ample opportunities to lie about in the sun. The U.S. Coast Guard Station is situated at the far end of the island, and in between are grassy stretches shaded by palm trees.

Plan ahead so you can enjoy the views: Bring a quilt, a jug of lemonade, and some fresh fruit. Settle yourselves in a pretty spot and let the nearby ocean serenade you.

As long as the weather stays fair (or if it's merely cloudy), leave the fort and cross the narrow two-lane bridge that connects Cockspur Island and Fort Pulaski to Highway 80. When you reach Highway 80,

Salt-Marsh Scenery

On the Bull River, the scenery is just as beautiful and the bottle-nosed dolphins are just as playful as they are near the Atlantic Ocean. You and your companion will squeal when **Low Country River Excursions** (8005 Highway 80 East at the Bull River Marina; 912–898–9222; $15; $12 for seniors) takes you on a leisurely adventure through the salt-marsh creeks. You'll enjoy ninety minutes of smooth riding aboard a 40-foot pontoon boat (Nature's Way or Dolphin's Dream). Daily departures are at noon, 2:00, 4:00, and 6:00 P.M. during the summer months; 2:00 and 4:00 P.M. during April; 2:00 and 6:00 P.M. Monday through Thursday from September 16 to October 15; and 2:00 P.M. only from October 16 to November 30. Reservations are recommended, and fun is guaranteed!

drive east, toward the Atlantic Ocean. Cross the Lazaretto Creek Bridge, which hovers over a small village and fleet of shrimp boats, and **Captain Mike's Dolphin Tours** (Lazaretto Creek; 912–786–5848 or 800–242–0166) will be to your right. A hand-painted sign signals your turn for this fun-filled boat tour. Drive down the bumpy road that once served as the only link to Tybee Island, appropriately called Old U.S. 80.

The afternoon sun usually warms the creek, and this operator's small tour boats venture out, weather permitting, into the river within an arm's length of playful dolphins. Enjoy a ride on the thatched-roof boats ($12 for adults) and marvel as the dolphins leap near. At times, they may even come within touching distance. Be patient! Captain Mike says to "count on an hour but plan for ninety minutes" depending on where the dolphins are playing.

Dolphin antics continue even after the tour ends. Cross the creek by car (heading west toward Savannah) via the Lazaretto Creek Bridge. Park along the palm-lined roadway leading to the public dock (just to your left after you cross the bridge) and prepare to feast your eyes on a spontaneous wonder of nature as schools of playful dolphins frolic in their natural habitat right before your eyes. The secret of this delightful water show is shared only by a few locals, so don't be surprised if you find yourselves alone on the pier. There are no admission fees, no time limits, and no trainers, so stay as long as you like. (The pier closes at dark.)

DAY TWO: evening

Drive down Highway 80 East, toward the beach, and turn left at Polk Road. At the next block turn right onto Fort Avenue. Proceed a block to Van Horn Drive and turn left again. Park just past the police station on Van Horn and head straight over the wooden walkway that leads to the beach and the splendor of the setting sun.

Stroll the beach at sunset, and you may meet only the tracks of loggerhead turtles that have dragged themselves up to the dunes to lay eggs. The serenity of this place is startling. A five-o'clock traffic hour on Tybee consists of a shrimp boat chugging into the river after a day at sea or a freighter following a pilot boat into the port of Savannah. A brisk ocean breeze blows continuously, and occasionally a wind surfer will dance along the waves, adding bright color to an otherwise lusterless ocean. As the sun sets, watch Savannah end its day against a backdrop of vivid orange.

Even if you leave the beach after sunset, you may be reluctant to call it a day. A late dinner is the perfect excuse for burning the midnight oil. Return to the Ocean Plaza to shower away the sand, but don't get too dressed up. Remember, you're on Tybee.

DINNER

The owners of the popular North Beach Grill took their success a step further with **Georges'** (1105 East Highway 80; 912–786–9730; expensive), a newer eatery that is making headlines. With wood-planked ceilings and hardwood floors resembling the interior of an old Tybee beach house, Georges' offers an atmosphere that is subdued after dark, with tables dimly lit and soft music playing. An intimate bar and comfortable seating are available if you have to wait, but owing to the restaurant's sudden popularity, reservations are suggested. The eighty-eight-seat restaurant features a menu reflective of "American fusion," according to owner George Jackson, and combines an Asian influence with a sprinkle of the Old South. Especially enticing is the sautéed fresh fish (halibut, grouper, or sea bass, depending on availability) over ragout of tasso ham and lima beans with Vidalia onion puree and sweet corn vinaigrette. The desserts are all homemade—the chocolate torte alone is worth the trip. If you are seeking a view, you won't find it here. This tiny eatery is located alongside a busy highway, but if you dine after dark it won't really matter. For romance, atmosphere, and a meal worthy of Savannah's finest, Georges' is the place to treat yourselves well during a stay on Tybee.

Return to the Ocean Plaza and toast the day from your oceanside deck. Tip palmfuls of soothing aloe vera lotion into your hands and smooth it across each other's sun-caressed shoulders. The extra moisture will ready your skin for more Tybee Island sun tomorrow.

DAY THREE: morning

BREAKFAST

Your last day on Tybee arrives despite all your efforts to delay the inevitable. Check out of the Ocean Plaza and walk over to the **Sunrise Restaurant** (1511 Butler Avenue; 912–786–7473; inexpensive) for breakfast. The chef's signature hash browns with diced ham, onions, and broccoli are a tasty complement for omelettes made any way you desire.

After breakfast, the **Tybee Island Marine Science Center** (Fourteenth Street Parking Lot; 912–786–5917) is the place to start the day's adventures. Just yards from the sand, the center features aquariums containing species found along coastal Georgia. Guided beach walks and seinings (dragging the ocean bottom with a net) are available, as are tours, classes, and lectures. Beachcombers can even bring in sea treasures found on the beach for identification.

Next stop is the **Tybee Market IGA** (1111 Butler Avenue; 912–786–4601), where you'll pick up some cheese and fruit for a midmorning snack and some sandwiches for a picnic lunch. Pack your goodies so they are easy to carry and head back to North Beach, where you explored yesterday morning.

Conveniently situated at the north end of the beach is the **Tybee Island Lighthouse and Museum** (30 Meddin Drive; 912–786–5801). Schedules vary by season, so call ahead for hours. Memorabilia ranging from Civil War relics to personal writings of songwriter Johnny

Mercer are among the displays in the museum. Spend some time here, then climb the stairs to the top of the beautiful lighthouse. The panoramic deck at the top offers an outstanding view of the Atlantic Ocean and Hilton Head Island. Georgia's oldest lighthouse (built in 1736 and rebuilt in 1867), the Tybee Island beacon stands 154 feet high and is one of the most pho-tographed lighthouses in the country.

Descend the stairs and take your picnic sandwiches to the park near the light-house. Soon you'll be on your way, so now's your chance to plan your return. If this visit was a summer fling, make a reserva-tion to return in the fall—the most delightful time of the year to spend a weekend at the beach. Uncluttered, with few crowds, the oceanfront will seem romantically desolate, as if just you two had the world to yourselves.

Love Light

It's no secret: Tybee Island's most beloved romantic attraction is its lighthouse, the oldest and tallest of the two functioning light stations that remain of the original fifteen on the Georgia coast. The rays of light from its Fresnel lens can be seen by lonely mariners as far as 18 miles out to sea. The views of the ocean from its observation deck have sparked many a romance and prompted hundreds of wedding ceremonies on the island's shores.

DINNER

You can't leave Tybee Island without stopping off at one of its most treasured eateries—where "the elite eat in their bare feet." As you're driving off the island on Highway 80 west, turn left at the rustic arrow-shaped CRAB SHACK sign that will appear on your right. The winding road is called Chimney Creek, a rather eclectic street with old Tybee clapboard houses, new brick homes, broken-down cars, mobile homes on stilts, and tiny docks that link to a charming creek. When the road ends, you'll find yourself giggling as your car stops at the rustic **Crab Shack** (Chimney Creek, Tybee Island; 912–786–9857; moderate). Don't let looks deceive you! This place has hosted the rich and famous (in their bare feet) and travel writers who rave about it in food articles published in magazines all over the world. From Clint Eastwood to John Travolta, the Crab Shack has become famous among locals and tourists. Unless you arrive by 6:30 P.M., you'll wait about an hour for a table. Voted as serving "Savannah's Best Seafood," this is the place to come with a sunburn and sand between your toes. Tank tops aren't just acceptable here, they're the recommended attire.

A wooden deck supports round tables with holes cut in the center (that's where you dump your shells). All the food is boiled or steamed shellfish and is served on throwaway plates. The beer is cold and the margaritas are frosty. If you choose to dine outside, you'll land somewhere under the massive branches of hundred-year-old live oaks, accented with tropical foliage and surrounded by twinkling lights that are strung overhead.

Fashioned after Gilligan's grass hut, the inside eating area is just as entertaining. The windows are all open and the view of the creek is splendid. Visit the sexy bar in the rear of this dock house and peer through a crack in the floor to see the creek below. If it happens to be raining the evening of your visit, take a few minutes to snuggle up at the bar as the water drops off the metal roof. Imagine you're stranded in the grass hut of a village deep in the jungles of Africa. Then order a platter of the Crab Shack's sampler and crack away at the night!

Before you stroll out to your car, pop into the attached **Gift Shack,** which is exactly what you'll find—a shack filled with some of Savannah's most unusual coastal-themed gift items. From Arthur Court Serveware and John Perry sculptures to Polonaise ornaments and Blue Mist pewter, you'll leave with an armful! Let your mate shop away; this is one place you won't want to forget!

FOR MORE ROMANCE

If you're a high roller, don't hesitate to board the *Atlantic Star* (Lazaretto Creek Pier, turn right off U.S. 80 just after you cross the Lazaretto Creek Bridge; 912–786–7827; $9.95 per person), a casino cruise boat that takes you from Tybee Island out into the Atlantic Ocean for Las Vegas–style blackjack, and slot playing. The boat is small but clean and, weather permitting, leaves Lazaretto Creek on Saturday at 1:00 P.M., returning at 5:00 P.M., or at 7:00 P.M., returning at 11:00. Weekdays, the *Star* sails from 7:00 to 11:00 P.M., weather permitting. Though the four-hour cruise is not recommended for those prone to motion sickness, you should know that some gamblers have returned to land with heavy pockets.

On a Tybee Island Friday night, nothing could be more romantic than to travel back in time to a small-town pastime: bingo! Head for the lighthouse (you'll see it towering over the island) and about a block south of its base you'll find a nostalgic clapboard building that boasts a large American flag. You'll discover locals gathering at the **American Legion Hall** (Fort Screven; no telephone number; inexpensive), where the stakes aren't too high but the fun is plentiful. You'll forget all about the telephone, fax machines, and the Internet here. When the caller grasps the ball and calls out a number, you and your loved one might just be the lucky ones.

For true solitude, the **Hunter House Inn** (1701 Butler Avenue; 912–786–7515; $75 to $125) boasts an uncluttered beach-house atmosphere, with a sprawling front porch dotted with rocking chairs. A stay here offers afternoon cocktails, an opportunity to dine in the inn's acclaimed restaurant (one of Tybee's finest), and a perfect place to meet interesting out-of-towners, if you are so inclined.

Fun Love in the Sun

A Hilton Head Respite

ROSS THE SAVANNAH RIVER BRIDGE to the South Carolina Low Country and discover the surprises that await on Hilton Head Island. Amid the quiet of these sanctuaries and steady ocean breezes, love will bloom like the sails of a wind-touched schooner. The forty-minute drive to Hilton Head Island from Savannah is truly exhilarating and offers a taste of the tropics.

PRACTICAL NOTES: Drive your own car or a rental from one of the agencies at the airport for your trek to Hilton Head, being sure to call ahead to rent an oceanside villa at the island's Palmetto Dunes resort.

DAY ONE: morning

It's about a forty-minute drive to Hilton Head Island from Savannah. Take Oglethorpe Avenue west to the Eugene Talmadge Memorial Bridge and head north across the river into South Carolina. About 5 miles past the bridge, bear right onto Alternate S.C. Highway 170. Drive about 6 miles until you reach S.C. Highway 46 and turn right onto this road. About 12 miles down you'll come to U.S. 278, which will lead you directly onto the island.

DAY ONE: afternoon

LUNCH

Plan to arrive on the island in time for lunch at **Signe's Heaven Bound Bakery & Cafe** (93 Arrow Road, Hilton Head; 843–785–9118;

Romance AT A GLANCE

◆ *Feed your loved one a little taste of heaven at* **Signe's Heaven Bound Bakery & Cafe** *(93 Arrow Road, Hilton Head; 843–785–9118).*

◆ *Stock up on supplies for your overnight stay at a unique, open-air market,* **Harris Teeter** *(Office Park Road; 843–785–6185).*

◆ *Sleep in the dunes—***Palmetto Dunes** *(4 Queen Folly Road, Hilton Head; 800–845–6130), that is—a luxury resort that will hypnotize you and your companion.*

◆ *Explore the many nature trails of the island or bike through the wonderland of trails.*

◆ *Bring your binoculars and handbook to study the wide array of birds found in the area.*

◆ *Share little bits of food at* **Tapas Restaurant** *(11 Northbridge Plaza, Hilton Head; 843–681–8590).*

◆ *Soak up the moon rays over the Atlantic Ocean and stroll the beach for a storybook ending to your day.*

moderate), a delightful eatery where gourmet coffees, teas, and desserts complement a healthful menu of "super salads" (including delicious chicken tarragon and tuna fish salads) and sandwiches (try the Hot Popeye, a homemade sourdough roll filled with spinach, mushrooms, onions, tomatoes, cream cheese, and Monterey Jack cheese). The bakery is open 8:00 A.M. to 4:00 P.M. during the week and 9:00 A.M. to 2:00 P.M. on Saturday. It's closed on Sunday. If you're there by 11:30 A.M., you can avoid the wait and find a table on the wooden deck. For dessert, feed each other a slice of heavenly cheesecake. Then seek out the sandy beaches and miles of quaint shops on Hilton Head Island.

Before checking into your villa, stop at **Harris Teeter** (Park Plaza Shopping Center, Office Park Road, Hilton Head; 803–785–6185), a bright, airy supermarket reminiscent of a roadside produce stand. Purchase fresh breads, fruit, cheese, and wine for snacks and breakfast during your overnight stay here.

Check into the oceanside villa you've reserved at **Palmetto Dunes** (4 Queen Folly Road, Hilton Head; 800–845–6130; $195 to $310 per night), a 2,000-acre resort where tennis is free and the sounds of the waves drenching the beach will lull you into a blissful trance. Rent a pair of bicycles—or a bicycle built for two—at the resort or at one of the island's numerous bike rental outlets. Bicycle rental rates are in the range of about $5.00 for an hour, $12.00 for a day, and $25.00 for a week. Spend the afternoon exploring Hilton Head's 14-plus miles of paved public bike trails. Many of the island's resort communities have additional bike paths—Palmetto Dunes is among them. Ask for a map of the whole system at the front desk before you head out for the afternoon. If bicycles aren't your style, the hotel also rents motorboats, canoes, and in-line skates.

DAY ONE: evening
DINNER

If you are not exhausted from the afternoon's excursions, take an early evening stroll on the beach and watch the sun set. Then shower and dress for an exotic dining experience at the **Tapas Restaurant** (11 Northridge Plaza, Hilton Head; 843–681–8590; moderate). Spanish for "little bits," tapas are appetizer-size, snack-like dishes served in succession to make a complete meal—perfect for sharing. Wine is available by the glass or bottle. Menu items, which range in price from $3.50 to $8.95, include scallops tempura, shrimp Parthenon, blackberry chicken, grilled pesto salmon, and Georgian pork.

With dinner behind you and the moonlit Atlantic Ocean just outside your villa, call it a day.

DAY TWO: morning
BREAKFAST

The morning sunlight will soon creep in through the windows to awaken you. Take time to lounge around during the early morning on your private porch, sipping coffee and sharing the breakfast treats you purchased yesterday.

The rest of the morning is wide open—you can laze around in the luxurious privacy of your villa, hit the links at one of the island's seventeen public golf courses (or one of the three Palmetto Dunes designer courses), or shop till you drop for lunch. **The Mall at Shelter Cove** (24 Shelter Cove Lane; 843–686–3090) is an enclosed shopping complex of fifty-five stores with famed anchor department stores at both ends.

DAY TWO: afternoon

LUNCH

The Village at Wexford shopping complex offers the perfect place for a romantic lunch. **Cafe at Wexford** (1000 William Hutton Parkway; 843–686–5969; inexpensive) capitalizes on country French decor to create an intimate ambience that complements its country French menu. Wood floors and warm-hued brickwork are a pleasing backdrop for such midday treats as veal sweetbreads, pâté de foie gras, and delicious fillets of fish encrusted with potato and onion. Reservations are suggested.

After lunch, your short visit to Hilton Head Island culminates with a dream cruise aboard the *Stars and Stripes,* the famous yacht that captured the America's Cup with Dennis Connor at its helm. Pickup is at Harbour Town (843–842–4155). Ninety-minute cruises leave daily at 2:30 and 4:30 P.M. and cost $24 per person; a sunset cruise leaves at 6:30 P.M. Senior Captain Rick Perry and his experienced crew will steer the two of you and your seagoing mates through the beautiful waters surrounding the island paradise. Then it's back to the mainland, and back down to earth.

FOR MORE ROMANCE

Lovebirds are truly in heaven on Hilton Head, where more than 250 species of birds are found. The best way to view the birds is to take a guided bird-watching tour by kayak. Offered daily whenever the weather permits, these tours bring you as close to nature as you can get. Call **Kayak Nature Trips** (at the Plaza at Shelter Cove, Hilton

Head; 843–686–6996, or at South Beach Marina, Hilton Head; 843–671–2643) or **Awesome Expeditions** (Shelter Cove Marina, Hilton Head; 843–842–9763).

It's Better in Beaufort

THE CAROLINA LOW COUNTRY

I F YOU THINK THE AMBIENCE OF SAVANNAH is overwhelming, imagine (and then experience) the South Carolina Low Country, where exquisite antebellum homes with massive columns and enticing verandas take you back to the days of Scarlett and Tara. Beaufort's warm salt breezes, shrimp boats, and sailing make this quaint seaside village a must-see "Savannah" attraction.

PRACTICAL NOTES: Beaufort is tiny; a day and a night are adequate to see the sights. Make reservations at the Best Western/Sea Island Inn and the Whitehall Plantation Restaurant.

DAY ONE: morning

Leave the mainland, bid farewell to Savannah, and head west for the salt marshes via I–16. Exit at I–95 North and drive until you reach the exit for Highway 46 to 170. Roll your windows down and breathe in the salty air as picturesque Highway 170 leads you to Beaufort. The forty-five-minute drive from Savannah and across the Broad River is a treat in itself. This two-lane road is graced on either side by soft marshes of green and gold, wispy white egrets, and gentle tides. Known as the South Carolina Low Country, this Southern paradise changes gloriously with the seasons and turns a myriad of colors when the sun sets. Slow down and savor the breezes as you pass tiny fishing boats bobbing slowly up and down and gulls swooping for their prey. Portions of *Forrest Gump, The Big Chill, The*

*R*om*a*n*ce*
AT A GLANCE

♦ *Spend an afternoon sitting in the **Henry C. Chambers Waterfront Park** feeding the pigeons as sailboats bob by and the water glistens like gold.*

♦ *Explore the living quarters of a merchant planter at the **John Mark Verdier House** (801 Bay Street, Beaufort; 843–524–6334) and discover other landmarks in this city by the sea before dining on Lady's Island at Whitehall Plantation Restaurant (27 Whitehall Drive; 843–521–1700).*

♦ *Discover eighteenth-century artifacts and industry in the beautiful **Beaufort Museum** (843–525–7077).*

♦ *Play with the dolphins as the sea comes alive on the **Islander** cruise (Waterfront Park, Beaufort; 843–671–5000) and view historic Beaufort by water.*

♦ *Enjoy dinner by sea at **The Bank Grill & Bar** (926 Bay Street; 843–522–8831).*

♦ *After a waterfront stroll, let the day end in the comfort of your room at the **Best Western/Sea Island Inn** (1015 Bay Street; 843–522–2090).*

Prince of Tides, and *Something to Talk About* were all filmed in the Low Country. Author Pat Conroy calls Beaufort his home and inspiration, and actor Tom Berenger extended his stay by purchasing a home here after filming *The Big Chill.*

Beaufort is located on an island called Port Royal, which is surrounded by several smaller islands (known as the South Carolina sea islands): Lady's Island, St. Helena Island, Parris Island, Cane Island, Gibbes Island, Distant Island, and Cat Island. The Beaufort River, where shrimp boats meander up and down throughout the day and festivals abound, runs east of the town and empties into the Atlantic Ocean.

When you reach Beaufort, stroll along the downtown **Henry C. Chambers Waterfront Park,** a picturesque park on the bay that includes a marina, a playground, swinging benches, and a lovely pathway for leisurely walks. A Farmer's Market is open in Waterfront Park on Wednesday and Saturday in season. Shrimp boats skim the waters while gulls perform antics around their wakes.

On the other side of the park is a downtown area that includes more than ninety historic homes. Following your jaunt along the waterfront, explore this extensive neighborhood. The entire 304

acres of the town have been designated a National Historic
Landmark District. Its stylish homes, accented with double porches,
have high ceilings, raised basements, and T-shaped floor plans for
maximum ventilation.

Visit the **John Mark Verdier House** (801 Bay Street, Beaufort;
843–524–6334). The Federal-style home, also known as the
LaFayette House, is characteristic of Beaufort architecture and is decorated to reflect the living quarters of a typical merchant planter
from 1790 through 1825. It is open for tours Tuesday through
Saturday from 11:00 A.M. to 4:00 P.M.; admission is $4.00 for adults.
Stand along Bay Street and envision the famous scene in 1825 when
the Marquis de Lafayette (who joined General George Washington
during the American Revolution) stood gallantly on the front steps
and addressed a crowd of onlookers.

Another downtown landmark not to miss is **St. Helena's
Episcopal Church** (501 Church Street, Beaufort). The oldest por-
tion of the church, which is bordered by Church, King, Newcastle,
and North Streets, dates from 1724. Expanded over the years, the
structure was eventually completed in the mid-1800s, although the
steeple was not added until the twentieth century. The sanctuary was
once used as a Union hospital, and the gravestones in the adjacent
churchyard were used as tables for amputations. Sailors stationed
on the U.S.S. *New Hampshire* (a Federal warship) carved the ornate
altar. The church houses one of the most respected organs in
America—a Taylor and Booty Dutch-style instrument installed in
the 1890s. Mason Locke Weems, the man who is said to have con-
cocted the story of George Washington and the cherry tree, is buried
in the churchyard.

DAY ONE: afternoon

LUNCH

The South Carolina sea islands are all within minutes of Beaufort
and worthy of further exploration. Venture beyond downtown
Beaufort by driving on Highway 21 South across to Lady's Island
and the **Whitehall Plantation Restaurant** (27 Whitehall Drive,
Beaufort; 843–521–1700; moderate). Cross the Lady's Island Bridge
and take the first sharp right onto Whitehall Drive. This romantic
bayside eatery, specializing in contemporary Low Country cuisine,

overlooks a striking waterside glistening with all the details of a Pat Conroy novel—peaceful marshes, blue skies, and the salty scent of the Low Country. Order fresh seafood, veal steaks, lamb, and luscious flambé desserts. The restaurant is open Monday through Saturday for lunch from 11:30 A.M. to 2:30 P.M. and for dinner from 5:30 to 9:30 P.M. Brunch is served on Sunday from 11:00 A.M. to 2:00 P.M.

Sampling the history of Beaufort's waterfront requires the energy you won't have after dining at the Whitehall Plantation, so, as Southern tradition dictates, drive back to Beaufort to rest for an hour. The **Best Western/Sea Island Inn** (1015 Bay Street, Beaufort; 843–522–2090; $71 to $99) is a quaint, forty-three-room inn located on the site of an old hotel where Saturday night dances were held in a massive ballroom. Razed in 1960, the old hotel was replaced by the present structure, which has become the most popular place to stay in Beaufort due to its proximity to the waterfront park. The hotel boasts a traditional facade that blends in nicely with the surrounding historic homes and downtown shops and is a quiet, peaceful, clean place to stay for under a hundred dollars. Guests are also welcome to use an outdoor pool and to enjoy a complimentary continental breakfast in the morning.

Another charming lodging option is the **TwoSuns Bed & Breakfast** (1705 Bay Street; 800–532–4244; $105 to $135 per night). This unique house overlooking Beaufort Bay was once a home for Beaufort schoolteachers. Its six rooms are decorated in individual themes, from Oriental to Victorian. For a little something special, ask for Chamber D, where an original 1916 antique full-body shower awaits. Or enjoy a view of the bay from a shared screened porch in Chambers B and C. A third-floor room boasts renovated skylights for a view of the stars. Tea and toddies are served between 5:00 and 6:00 P.M. daily. For a preview of the TwoSuns, check out the inn's Web site: www.twosunsinn.com.

After your nap, head out to the **Beaufort Museum** (713 Craven Street, Beaufort; 843–525–7077). You'll find artifacts that document the rich history of this city that was first founded by the Spanish in 1514 and chartered by the British in 1711. Beaufort experienced prosperity in the eighteenth century as indigo and rice plantations thrived, and it also became a haven for the cotton industry. Within the museum are Native American artifacts, art, textiles, and Civil

War weapons. A lecture and slide show (every Friday at 10:30 A.M. March through October) about Beaufort's history give a good overview of the area. The museum is open from 10:00 A.M. to 5:00 P.M. every day except Wednesday, Sunday, and holidays. Admission is $2.00 for adults.

The remainder of the afternoon is designed to tease your senses. Hop aboard *Islander* **Cruises** (Waterfront Park, Beaufort; 843–671–5000; operated seasonally) and feel the warm sun and soft breeze against your skin. Watch the dolphins at play and the wading egrets savoring the wildlife appetizers along the shore. This relaxing cruise should put you in the spirit for a short siesta in your room.

DAY ONE: evening

DINNER

Rejuvenated by your snooze, you'll be ready to sally forth for dinner in the early evening. An authentic old bank in downtown Beaufort has been transformed into a restaurant and bar—**The Bank Grill & Bar** (926 Bay Street; 843–522–8831; moderate), overlooking the waterfront park and the Intracoastal Waterway. This multilevel eatery features an extended menu with more than a hundred items ranging from thick steaks to pastas and local seafood. Ask for a table upstairs if you're hoping for a glimpse of the water through the trees in the park.

After dinner, stroll down to the waterfront and swing to the melodies of the sea breeze. You may pass a couple of waterfront pubs, but nightlife is nearly nonexistent here. Instead of having a night on the town, relish this chance to enjoy a quiet, Old South evening. In the morning head back to the mainland and Savannah.

FOR MORE ROMANCE

Located just twenty minutes from downtown Beaufort is **Hunting Island State Park,** a tropical paradise with more than 125 species of birds, as well as a romantic lighthouse that is open to the public. With more than 5,000 acres and 200 campsites (40 of which may be reserved), a boardwalk, and nature trails, this peaceful island is a perfect place to visit during the summer. Reservations are recommended for campsites; call (843) 838–2011.

During your stay on Hunting Island, climb the stairs of the romantic lighthouse and then explore the island's new nature center. Admission to both is free.

For a more elegant, romantic, and costly stay in Beaufort, spend the night in the renowned **Rhett House Inn** (1009 Craven Street, Beaufort; 843–524–9030; $160 to $225 during the fall). Built in 1820, the inn is the former home of Thomas Rhett, one of five wealthy brothers. The prestigious B&B has been praised by travel writers from all over the world as one of the South's most luxurious and romantic places to stay.

A Tropical Paradise
LITTLE ST. SIMONS ISLAND

HE SCENARIO HAS BEEN CONTRIVED thousands of times: A couple is stranded on a deserted island. Except for the fiddler crabs burrowing in the sand and a gull or two soaring above the dunes, the beach is empty. Palm trees billow in the breeze, and the thick forest beyond is alive with colorful squawking birds and grazing wildlife.

This postcardlike scene seems more descriptive of a Caribbean island than a tiny, romantic destination off the coast of Georgia. But such a tropical paradise awaits at Little St. Simons Island, the northernmost and most secluded of the string known as the Golden Isles.

PRACTICAL NOTES: Make your reservations at the Lodge on Little St. Simons well in advance. The tiny resort limits the number of guests to thirty, and access to the private island is by reservation only. Bring insect repellent and sunscreen. Ferries leave from St. Simons Island at 10:30 A.M. and 4:30 P.M. daily. The departures from Little St. Simons Island to St. Simons Island are at 10:00 A.M. and 4:00 P.M. The ferry ride takes about fifteen minutes. Fares are included in your reservation fee.

DAY ONE: morning

BREAKFAST

Leave Savannah by 7:30 A.M. and head south. The Richmond Hill exit off I–95 South just a few miles down from Savannah offers a variety of fast-food eateries for a quick cup of coffee or pastry. To stay on schedule and not risk missing the boat, make your stop a quick one. Then proceed ninety minutes south of Savannah, down I–95 to exit 7 at St. Simons Island.

Romance AT A GLANCE

◆ Breathe the sea air as a ferry takes you to a secluded getaway at the **Lodge on Little St. Simons Island** (Little St. Simons Island; 912–638–7472 or 888–733–5774).

◆ Experience unadulterated serenity at a rustic island sanctuary.

◆ Venture into the woods with your guide to study the various species of birds that make this island their home.

◆ Take an afternoon ride by horseback and spend the evening on the porch of the lodge as night falls.

◆ Fly-fish with a guide or surf cast for redfish, sea trout, and other game fish.

◆ Stroll more than 7 miles of secluded beaches, gathering an abundance of unique seashells.

◆ Spend an afternoon lying by an oversize swimming pool filled with spring water!

◆ Canoe through the island's many waterways and get a firsthand look at nature in action.

Little St. Simons Island is accessible only by boat. The ferry is docked at the **Hampton River Club Marina** (1000 Hampton River Club Drive, St. Simons Island; 912–638–1210). To reach it, cross the F. J. Torras Causeway and turn left at the first light (Sea Island Road) or go straight to the next light (Frederica Road). Then drive north on Frederica Road to the fork, where you'll bear right. (At this point Frederica changes to Lawrence Road.) Stay on this main road until you get to the fork at Hampton Plantation. Bear right again and then go straight until you see the guard house. Turn right just before the guard house, at the sign for the marina, and then right again onto the gravel road at the marina.

Park where you see AUTO PARKING signs. The boat slip is the first one at the dock. The ferry departs at 10:30 A.M. Your getaway officially begins once you arrive at the dock, where friendly staff members from the Lodge on Little St. Simons Island will be on hand to greet you and load your luggage onto the ferry.

DAY ONE: afternoon

The sun and surf, combined with the refreshing breeze, will make your short cruise not only scenic but exhilarating. Once you reach the island, other lodge staff members will be standing by, awaiting your arrival. Your luggage will be transported to the lodge, and after a fifteen-minute orientation, you'll be free to roam about. Check into the **Lodge on Little St. Simons Island** (912–638–7472 or 888–733–5774; $325 to $525). A bit rough-looking on the outside, the 1917 lodge has wood-paneled walls bearing antlers and deer heads on the inside. Check in and then check out your accommodations. The Hunting Lodge (the main building) houses two comfortable rooms, each with twin beds, private bath, and air-conditioning. Michael Cottage, at the edge of the forest, has two bedrooms with a queen and twin beds, a private bath, living room with fireplace, large screened porch, and air-conditioning.

LUNCH

Have a delicious home-cooked lunch in the dining room, then settle in for a few minutes of exploring. You'll be enchanted by Mother Nature's elaborate display of wealth. This 10,000-acre island offers the perfect getaway for couples who are seeking the solitude of the beach in a rustic, romantic setting without the inconveniences of camping—or the need for a passport. The sheer silence of the island, disturbed only by the clamor of nesting black skimmers, is remarkable. Rimmed by salt marshes and ocean-swept beaches, the setting has all the makings of a tropical paradise. In fall black-throated blue warblers dot

Birds of a Feather

Apart from the graceful, more aesthetically appealing birds you might observe during your stay on Little St. Simons, there are those who prefer matrimony and child-rearing habits that are typical of devoted featherless couples. During the spring the male marsh hawk engages in acrobatics designed to attract even the most inattentive female. Diving and swooping, this daring entertainer will find his mate, and then the two will begin construction of an orderly, foot-wide nest of grass, stems, and twigs at ground level and set up housekeeping. The bluish eggs will hatch in the cozy nest, and Mama and Papa will care for the tiny chicks for more than a month. The family will reside on the island until spring and then travel back up north.

the forest with color. Red knots numbering between 4,000 and 10,000 shower the shoreline with grand choreography. You may spot a short-eared owl or an egret soaring over a field of sweetgrass or a turtle on its upward path over a massive cedar stump. European fallow deer may pick their way through the same trails you wander. The soft serenade of wildlife and occasional conversation of guests and employees is all you'll hear in this Southern oasis. No televisions or telephones invade your privacy.

All guests with reservations are welcome to sample any wildlife activities free of charge as part of their stay at the lodge. Guided trail rides are offered Wednesday through Sunday, twice daily; other options, including fishing, boating, canoeing, nature tours, and bird-watching, are offered upon demand by a majority of the guests. (For instance, if five guests prefer fishing, fishing will be the tour of the day. If the guests prefer bird-watching, then that activity will be offered.)

Spend your first afternoon testing (or showing off) your equestrian skills as a guide leads you on horseback along a maze of riding trails. Upon your return, relax in a rocker on the lodge porch and sip a glass of iced tea before heading in for a nap and shower.

DAY ONE: evening

DINNER

Contemplate the sunset from the front porch of the lodge as your dinner feast is prepared. There will be more than you can eat, so don't snack during the day. Served family-style, the hearty meals are likely to include such Southern-style fare as fresh fish, fried chicken, barbecue, home-baked breads, and pecan pie.

When the bowl-passing is over, settle down to the silence of the evening. Murmur sweet promises to one another in the shade of a 300-year-old live oak. When the setting sun sinks beneath the marsh-rimmed horizon, catch a falling star, or just be.

DAY TWO: morning

BREAKFAST

Awaken in the morning to sounds of nature and rise for a full breakfast, again served family-style in the dining room.

Your morning can be spent lounging on the beach or rocking on the porch, depending on your fondness for the sun. The beach is completely desolate and unspoiled, and the surf is usually mild. If you choose to lie about on this "private" island with your love, take along a picnic lunch that the chef will be pleased to prepare for your outing. Porch-sitters can enjoy fresh fruit and snacks available throughout the day in the lodge.

Lunch Under the Live ☆Oaks

Just when breakfast at the Lodge on Little St. Simons Island seems like a blissful dream (peach pecan pancakes, grits with tasso gravy, hot apple cereal, and homemade buttermilk biscuits), the chef will set a colorful table beneath the live oaks and you'll be introduced to a great Southern tradition: the lowcountry boil. Local blue crabs with red pepper sauce, sausage, fresh corn, potatoes, and shrimp intermingle with the salty coastal air, giving you something to rave about back home.

Afternoon happy hours are happiest on the front lawn when oysters (in season) are roasted beneath the hundred-year-old grand oaks. On many occasions, Captain Doug cranks up and blue crabs, cheese and crackers, and fresh shrimp are the cocktail hour fare. Wow!

To top off the lodge's romantic options, a monthly full-moon beach picnic entices guests with baskets of blue crabs or lowcountry boil. You'll enjoy your meal in a pavilion that overlooks a 7-mile stretch of pristine, deserted beach.

DAY TWO: afternoon

Walk on the wild side this afternoon. Take your companion's hand and set out on a guided bird-watching tour (after you've lobbied with the other guests for this activity). More than 220 species of bird have been spotted on the island. Tours explore the north end (the oldest part) of the island, where participants learn about the centuries-old forests and wetland ecosystems.

Go for a swim in the pool, filled with spring water, before you pack up and head back to the mainland on the 4:00 P.M. ferry. Maybe you'll want to make a reservation to return next year.

FOR MORE ROMANCE

Twice a year, the lodge welcomes an Orvis-endorsed instructor to teach a two-day fly-fishing course. Cast a rod in tidal creeks and surf and land redfish, speckled trout, and flounder. Instruction is geared toward all skill levels.

Day visits to the island are available by reservation only on Tuesday and Wednesday only. A $75 per person admission includes boat transportation, a tour with a naturalist, and lunch at the lodge, as well as time out on the beach.

Love in the "Wilderness"
A Cumberland Island Retreat

UMBERLAND ISLAND NATIONAL SEASHORE is for lovers seeking haunting beauty and the sense of being truly alone in an undiscovered tropical paradise. The Atlantic Ocean empties its fury onto the beaches of this barrier island, and the waves leave hundreds of delicate seashells as gifts for beachcombers. Here you can escape the world while relishing miles of untouched shoreline. You can stroll for miles without meeting a soul, and the island offers but a single inn for your escape. Sleep with Mother Nature tapping on your window and dine like royalty.

PRACTICAL NOTES: Call the Greyfield Inn to make reservations well in advance of your visit. For registered guests the inn provides a private ferry, the *Lucy R. Ferguson,* which leaves Fernandino Beach Harbor from Amelia Island at 9:30 A.M. and 12:15 and 5:30 P.M. Cumberland Island has no stores, so be sure to bring any special dietary requirements, sunblock, film, and prescription or over-the-counter medications with you.

DAY ONE: morning

If you're an early riser and plan to make the first ferry at 9:30 A.M., leave Savannah by 6:30 to allow ample time. Stop at one of the fast-food eateries along the interstate for pastries and coffee on the run. If you'd rather sleep in, you can still make one of the two later ferries. Take I–16 west from downtown Savannah to I–95 south. Leave the highway at exit 129 and bear left onto Atlantic Drive. Proceed about 15 miles to Fernandino Beach. Atlantic Drive changes to Center Street. Turn left onto Center Street and proceed to the Fernandino

◆ Let the ferry transport you to a dream world at the **Greyfield Inn** (8 North Second Street, P.O. Box 900, Fernandina Beach, Florida 32035-0900; 904–261–6408) on a private island.

◆ Spend your days combing the land for shark's teeth, fishing, shelling, clam digging, swimming, or hiking.

◆ Dine as the sun sets, enjoying the fresh flowers and candlelight set before you and your companion.

◆ Explore a library that contains a private collection and many one-of-a-kind books once belonging to the Carnegie family.

◆ Study the hundred-year-old live oaks that grace the lawn of the inn as you swing on the porch of this highly acclaimed mansion.

◆ Stand in the surf and try your luck at fishing on a beach that is nearly deserted.

Beach Harbor and the ferry. You may want to bring a light snack (purchased from any of the various fast-food eateries you'll pass as you exit I–95). The ferry ride over takes about forty-five minutes.

Check in at the **Greyfield Inn** (904–261–6408; $275 to $450 for rooms; restaurant, expensive), which offers quiet accommodations in a century-old Carnegie family summer retreat. Rooms in this three-story plantation mansion are cozy, simple, rustic (in a Carnegie sort of way), and extremely serene.

DAY ONE: afternoon

Unpack your bags, then spend the afternoon exploring the island. Only 16 miles long and 3 miles wide at its broadest point, Cumberland is the largest of the nine barrier islands that keep the Georgia shoreline from being totally exposed to the Atlantic. Once the home of the Timicuan Indians and later the site of Spanish forts and missions, this island was also where two forts were built by General James Oglethorpe. Oglethorpe's hunting lodge (called Dungeness) was the only home here, and the island was left pretty much uninhabited until it was purchased by Revolutionary War hero Nathanael Greene and his wife, Catherine. A new mansion, also named Dungeness, was built in 1786 to accommodate the family, who logged the island's live oaks for use in the construction of navy ships. When the home burned down nearly one hundred years later, the Greenes abandoned the island, which was purchased in 1882 by the Thomas Carnegie family. Hence began an era of wealth on the island, where fishing, hunting, swimming, polo, and fencing became new pastimes. Today 80 percent of the island is owned and managed by the National Park Service, with the remainder still in the hands of the Carnegie family heirs.

LUNCH

The Greyfield Inn chef will pack a picnic lunch for you to take on a beach trip or on an exploration through the woods. If you opt for the latter, be prepared to meet wild horses, deer, squirrels, rabbits, and maybe even an otter. You'll stumble across the remains of the third Dungeness, the fifty-nine-room mansion of Andrew Carnegie. It burned down in 1959, but if you close your eyes, you can visualize its former palatial grandeur. Chimneys and other remnants still stand. Among other ruined structures nearby is Tabby House, the oldest home on the island, which once served as housing for the gardeners of the estate. Enjoy your picnic among the remnants and imagine ladies in evening gowns whirling with tuxedo-clad gents.

Nuptials of the Rich and Famous

One of this country's most famous couples, the late Mr. and Mrs. John F. Kennedy Jr., chose Cumberland Island as the site of their nuptials in 1996. Their choice was inspired by the beauty of the island as well as its privacy. They wed in a tiny African Baptist church that is nothing more than a small shack and spent their first night as husband and wife in the Greyfield Inn.

DAY ONE: evening

In the early evening, sip wine from the inn's extensive selection and catch the sunset and ocean breeze from the front porch. You can lie flat (both of you!) on a wonderful porch swing and listen as nature's own symphony orchestra warms up.

DINNER

Dining at Greyfield is an experience in itself! You'll feel as if you've been invited to an elegant dinner party at the home of a wealthy friend. There are no private tables here, but with candlelight, fresh flowers, and a grand island sunset, simply gaze into the eyes of your mate for a private conversation! At a more formal meal (coat and tie for men), the inn's nightly entree consists of fresh seafood, Cornish game hen, lamb, or beef tenderloin, along with homemade breads, fresh vegetables, and delightful desserts. The wine list is superb, and the inn maintains a well-stocked bar if you're interested in an after-dinner liqueur. The bar, located in the mansion's former gun room, is operated on an "honest John" system, so help yourself but be sure to maintain your integrity.

DAY TWO: morning

It's no wonder celebrities flock to the Greyfield Inn to escape. There is, perhaps, no other place in the world quite so adorned with natural beauty and extravagant furnishings for those who seek time to do nothing.

If you've selected a master bedroom (with a beautiful antique king-size bed and private sitting room), you'll awaken to the sounds of absolutely nothing except an occasional song from a bird. The sun will peek through the open windows and the illuminated live oaks, dripping with morning sunlight, will capture your fancy. As you gaze at the splendor of this new morning, you'll feel hypnotized as if you're observing a Renoir painting—soft and bursting with pastels!

Arise and put on your flip-flops. The beach is alive with life that has settled in small ponds and puddles that bubble beneath your toes. There is a fresh covering of foam remaining from last night's waves and if your eyes wander, you will see absolutely no one. On some days, you'll thrill to the sight of wild horses galloping by. On other mornings, giant horseshoe crabs and chattering gulls may be your only company.

Travel the long, vacant, unpaved road back to the inn. If you would like to shower, there's a tiny bathhouse in the backyard, overlooking a beautiful waterway. There are overgrown adirondack chairs grouped near the bathhouse so while you're scrubbing away, your mate can ponder life as it was for Lucy and Thomas Carnegie's daughter, Margaret Ricketson, for whom the house was built.

BREAKFAST

Sumptuous breakfasts are served at the inn from 8:30 to 9:30 A.M. and include pancakes with blueberries and cream cheese; French toast; and egg omelettes, such as the popular Mexican-style omelette. Freshly squeezed orange juice and hot coffee are plentiful. Take your time—and take your cue from the unhurried staff. Their relaxed lifestyle is something you might want to bring back to the mainland.

After breakfast ask the chef to fill a bag with lots of beverages, sandwiches, and fruit. The beach is your destination today. Spend the rest of the morning relaxing together on the beach—enjoying the views, splashing in the waves, and feeding each other from the items in your lunch bag.

DAY TWO: afternoon

As an alternative to more beaching, you can take a three- to four-hour Jeep tour of the island with a naturalist or, if you prefer, you can bike around the island on your own. Both the tour and the bike rentals can be arranged by the Greyfield Inn for no additional charge. You're likely to see wild deer, huge sea turtles along the beach, and an occasional wild boar. Bird-watching is also great on Cumberland Island, which is home to elegant egrets and other seabirds. Binoculars are furnished by the inn, and a guide is available upon request.

Before you pack up and head back to the ferry in time for its 4:00 P.M. departure, stop at the reception desk and book a night for late October, when the breezes will be brisk and the surf capped with foam.

FOR MORE ROMANCE

For a mere $4.00 per night per person, you and your love can camp out under the stars on Cumberland Island. This very rustic getaway includes restrooms with showers. Primitive sites are available (no shower, no rest room) for $2.00 per night. You'll have to bring everything you might need. No grocery or camp supply stores are on the island. Besides food and camping gear, tops on your must-have list should be bug spray and sunscreen. Insects and snakes are prevalent during the warmer months, and sand gnats emerge during the spring and fall. Chiggers and ticks are found in high-grass areas from April to October, and alligators may be present at all times (although they have rarely been known to attack humans). If you choose this camping option, you'll cruise to the island on *The Cumberland Queen,* which leaves from St. Marys at 9:00 and 11:45 A.M. daily. Reservations are required, and the adult round-trip fare is $10.17 per person. During the off-peak season (October through February), the ferry does not run on Tuesday or Wednesday. To reach the ferry, take I–95 South from Savannah and turn off at exit 2, St. Marys and Folkston (Highway 40). Follow the signs to **Crooked River State Park,** approximately 10 miles from the interstate, rest a spell, and then venture onward on the same road to Cumberland Island National Seashore. Turn right onto St. Marys Street and you'll see the National Park Service building, where you'll need to get on a waiting list for *The Cumberland Queen.* All island visitors, whether staying overnight or not, must pay a $4.00 per person use fee.

It is *essential* to make reservations early (no walk-ins); call the **Cumberland Island National Seashore** (912–882–4335) to reserve a campsite and a place on the ferry. Set up your tent and then head down to the beach with chairs in hand. Let the day begin with the sun and end with the stars.

Doin' the Charleston
SLEEPOVER IN SOUTH CAROLINA

AVANNAHIANS LIKE TO BOAST that their city is more industrious, more beautiful, and more enchanting than Charleston. Charlestonians, in turn, claim that their city is more aristocratic, is far superior as a working port, and offers more to do in a compact area than Savannah. Surprisingly, Savannahians like to escape to Charleston, and Charlestonians, in turn, to Savannah, and you can decide for yourself. So this tale of two cities will take its turn with a two-day trip. Your romantic drive through the South Carolina Low Country and a couple of days spent browsing the shops of Charleston are a wonderful accompaniment to your stay in Savannah. When the day is done, you'll have not only recharged your souls but also formed your own opinions about these two historic cities. You may even pick up a bit of a drawl.

PRACTICAL NOTES: Make reservations at Magnolias and at the Mills House Hotel before leaving Savannah.

DAY ONE: morning

BREAKFAST

Before leaving Savannah early (plan to leave by 8:00 A.M.), have breakfast at the **Hyatt Regency Savannah's Windows** (2 West Bay Street, Savannah; 912–238–1234; moderate). A freshly made omelette or a stack of homemade buttermilk pancakes will complement your view of the shimmering Savannah River.

◆ *Stock up on a stack of buttermilk pan-cakes from the* **Hyatt Regency Savannah's Windows** *(2 West Bay Street; 912–238–1234) restaurant then gas up the car for a scenic drive up U.S. 17 north to Charleston, Savannah's sister city.*

◆ *"Do the Charleston," as they say, in the* **City Market** *area, where vendors offer everything from gourmet food items to pottery and jewelry.*

◆ *Dine in Southern charm at* **Magnolias** *(185 East Bay Street, Charleston; 843–577–7771) where old favorites like squash casserole and sweetened iced tea come in endless quantities.*

◆ *Take a leisurely carriage ride through this historic city in one of the most reputable carriage companies,* **Palmetto Carriage Works** *(843–723–8145).*

◆ *Sip on a cold refreshment and watch the crowd pass by at* **Henry's** *(City Market; 843–723–4363), a pub that's survived hurricanes.*

◆ *Check into the* **Mills House Hotel** *(115 Meeting Street; 843–577–2400), an outstanding lodge with period antiques and amenities like fluffy terry robes.*

◆ *Toast the evening at* **Club Habana** *(177 Meeting Street; 843–853–5008) where you might just be tempted to salute Charleston with a fine cigar!*

Drive out of town on I–16 West to I–95 North and proceed until you reach the Charleston exit. Follow this mostly two-lane road (Highway 17) around shaded curves, over the salt marshes, and finally into this city that rivals Savannah in so many ways. When you reach the city (at about 10:30 A.M.), follow the signs into the downtown Historic District. You'll pass grand eighteenth-century homes with exquisitely manicured lawns, ornate churches with towering steeples, horse-drawn carriages laden with camera-toting tourists, and boutiques, antiques stores, and eateries. (Sounds a little like the city you just left, no?)

Charleston is a grand old lady who has withstood the forces of nature—from hurricanes to earthquakes to epidemics—and still maintained her dignity. Along the city streets you'll meet an eclectic crowd, from hat-wearing basketweavers practicing their craft to uni-formed Citadel cadets strolling the sidewalks. You'll run into Charlestonians (recognizable by their aristocratic accents) who have come downtown to shop and maybe even lovers like yourselves out to discover the unknown secrets of this popular city.

Park in an all-day lot ($5.00 to $10.00). You won't need to return to your car until you're loaded with packages.

When you reach the downtown **City Market** area (Market Street between Meeting and East Bay Streets, Charleston; open 9:00 A.M. until sunset), the activity will increase. A line of long, open-air brick buildings, formerly the slave market, marks the center of this bustling cluster of boutiques, restaurants, and pubs. Stroll through the market, where vendors' mellifluous dialects may lure you inside. Between the porticoes you'll see Charleston natives weaving straw baskets. Stop and chat with them—Charlestonians are gracious hosts. As you proceed from one end of the market to the other, you'll discover tables filled with crafts, flea market items, old books, clothing, bags of famous Charleston three-bean soup, and jewelry. Take a couple of hours to peruse the wares, but remember, you're headed for an exquisite lunch, so don't spoil your appetite.

DAY ONE: afternoon

LUNCH

Proceed to **Magnolias** (185 East Bay Street, Charleston; 843–577–7771; inexpensive), perhaps the city's most popular eatery. The restaurant is an institution in South Carolina. Adorned with wrought-iron and etched-glass accents, Magnolias carries out the Southern theme in its innovative menu, which features new twists on old favorites like squash, chicken, collard greens, and grits. If you're into traditional fare, opt for the Southern fried chicken, and if you're more daring, try the seared yellow grits cakes with tasso gravy and greens on the side. The iced tea is as sweet as your partner, so drink as much as you like.

A carriage tour is the best way to see the city on short notice, so if you have any packages, return to your car and store them. Various tour companies line both sides of City Market, and prices vary with each one. **Palmetto Carriage Works** (40 North Market Street, Charleston; 843–723–8145) is the city's oldest and offers a one-hour mule-drawn tour through the Historic District. Carriages leave every twenty minutes. Your driver will take you up and down the brick and cobblestone streets and past some of the most beautiful antebellum homes in the country, providing running commentary as you clip-clop along. Many early settlers to Charleston came from Barbados and the Caribbean and brought with them designs boasting high ceilings, massive porches, and elongated windows—architectural elements well suited to warm-weather climates.

When your driver returns you to the old slave market area, walk south 1 block to **Tommy Condon's** (160 Church Street, Charleston; 843–577–3818; inexpensive), a true Irish pub. You and your mate can enjoy an Irish ale on the covered outdoor deck or sit in the friendly bar area with the locals. Wainscoted walls, paintings of the old country, and hardwood floors enhance this charming eatery.

DAY ONE: evening

Check into a luxurious suite at the **Mills House Hotel** (115 Meeting Street, Charleston; 843–577–2400; $130 to $250), one of the city's most outstanding lodgings. With a classical, aristocratic atmosphere and sunny, cheerful rooms decorated with period antiques, Mills House also offers such amenities as thick, fluffy terry-cloth robes and slippers. This reconstructed 1853 Italianate hotel once hosted prestigious guests such as General Robert E. Lee and former President Theodore Roosevelt. It is within easy walking distance of the busy Historic District.

Postcard Portraits

Stroll toward the Cooper River and discover the beautiful **Waterfront Park,** *where porch swings sway and sailboats dot the horizon. A cruise-ship terminal is within walking distance, and the atmosphere is carefree. Share a sorbet purchased from a strolling vendor, or soak your feet in a fountain where children may be dancing in the spray.*

DINNER

Charlestonians pride themselves on traditional, well-known eateries such as your lunch stop, Magnolias, but there's a new breed in town offering exciting Southern cuisine prepared in New York fashion. Try **Anson** (12 Anson Street, Charleston; 843–577–0551; expensive), a lovely establishment that puts a contemporary spin on South Carolina Low Country favorites. Try the cashew-crusted grouper with champagne sauce or one of Savannah's favorite dishes, crispy, scored flounder with tangy apricot-shallot glaze.

After dinner, it's time to toast your get-away. Join the evening partiers at **Club Habana** (177 Meeting Street, Charleston; 843–853–5008), a trendy cigar bar that boasts as its specialty a mint julep martini. Then stroll back to your plush room at the Mills House Hotel. A rich chocolate treat has been placed on your pillow. This night is still young.

DAY TWO: morning

BREAKFAST

Don your matching robes and read the morning newspaper (which is, by the way, at your doorstep). Your freshly squeezed orange juice and breakfast banquet will arrive on silver platters with a simple ring of room service. A truly Southern staff offers gracious assistance at your every turn. Checking out will be the only agonizing part of your visit here.

Searching for Seafood

An enchanting drive across the Cooper River Bridge will lead you to Mount Pleasant's **Shem Creek**, a haven for seafood lovers. Open-air restaurants line the docks, and shrimp boats maneuver in and out of the marina. Select any one of these delicious eateries and settle in for a Bloody Mary and a broiled seafood platter. Nothing could be finer!

Before you leave your seaside hostess, return to the Battery (your carriage tour undoubtedly took you here), on the tip of the narrow peninsula where the Ashley and Cooper Rivers meet. Some of the most photographed mansions in the world face the harbor here. Park along the street and spend a few minutes surveying the old cannons, taking snapshots along the walk, and savoring your last moments in Charleston.

FOR MORE ROMANCE

Make your reservations well in advance for **Charleston's Spoleto Festival USA**, one of the world's largest arts festivals, which takes place during late May and early June. This has become one of the most popular festivals in the world. Composer Gian Carlo Menotti conceived the idea to produce two festivals simultaneously—one in Charleston and one in Italy. Both feature more than a hundred events, from opera and chamber music to theatrical works, dance, and symphonic concerts. Thousands of people from all over the world flock to Charleston for this internationally acclaimed festival. Local talent is highlighted during this same period and hosts its own Piccolo Spoleto festival. If you wish to attend a Spoleto event, it is best to call the Spoleto office (843–579–3100) and request a schedule for the upcoming festival or visit their outstanding Web site for current information at www.spoletousa.org. Choose your event, purchase your tickets, and then book your room well in advance, as vacancies are scarce during this time.

A Sporting Time

Working Up a Sweat
A Savannah Sports Sampler

HE SAVANNAH SPOTLIGHT IS BRIMMING with beauty, overflowing with mystery, and blossoming with great dining spots, but missing from the lineup are major-league teams and major-league action. You two can create some major-league action of your own at the wide array of sporting activities in the area.

Take a dip in a dome-covered pool or observe Olympians in training at the largest weight-lifting center in the United States. Take a sailing lesson in a lake at the center of Savannah's most popular recreational park. Don your favorite sports cap and check out minor-league baseball players waiting to be discovered. Split a hot dog as you watch the great American pastime, Savannah-style.

PRACTICAL NOTES: Enjoy the activities of this itinerary from early May through late August. Before you leave home, decide whether you two are going to be spectators or participants, and bring along the gear you'll need. Take along a cooler and a blanket for your picnic lunch. Bring sunscreen to the ballpark if you're attending a day game or gnat spray if it's a night game, as well as plenty of pocket change to enjoy the nostalgia and good eats of Grayson Stadium. Get a Savannah Sand Gnat schedule before your arrival by calling (912) 351–9150. Reservations are necessary at the Hampton Inn, as well as for sailing lessons from the Savannah Sailing Center.

Romance AT A GLANCE

♦ Start your morning at **The Sunrise Restaurant** (Savannah Centre at Hodgsen Memorial; 912–356–3388) where you'll dine on light omelettes and a special mix of broccoli, onions, ham, and potatoes. Share a booth and the morning newspaper over coffee and fresh orange juice.

♦ Check out the softball action at **Allen E. Paulson Softball Complex** (Skidaway Road; 912–351–3852) and pitch a ball or two to your mate.

♦ Show your love just how strong you really are at the **Paul Anderson– Howard Cohen Weightlifting Center** (7232 Varnedoe Drive; 912–351–3500) and catch true Olympians in training.

♦ Stroll hand-in-hand around **Lake Mayer Community Park** (Montgomery Crossroad and Sallie Mood Drive; 912–652–6786) and then try your luck fishing (making sure to bait the hook for your mate) in the lake that surrounds the beautiful park.

♦ Get ready for baseball action as the Savannah Sand Gnats play at **Grayson Stadium** (1401 East Victory Drive; 912–351–9150) and you and your companion can watch the game high above the field in the Gnats' very own Stadium Club.

♦ Follow the crowd to **Coach's Corner** (3016 East Victory Drive, Thunderbolt; 912–352–2933) where you and your date can cheer on your favorite sporting team or try your hand at a little trivia.

♦ Commune with nature and each other at the **Skidaway Island State Park** (52 Diamond Causeway; 912–598–2300) where fiddler crabs and sandpipers will lure you into the wilds.

DAY ONE: morning

BREAKFAST

Come to Savannah early in the day, especially if you are determined to try everything in this power-packed itinerary. **The Sunrise Restaurant** (Savannah Center at Hodgson Memorial; 912–356–3388; inexpensive), a delightful, centrally located breakfast eatery, is the perfect place to find a booth, the *Savannah Morning News*, and a homemade omelette, pancakes, or panfried hash browns with broccoli, onions, and ham. This locally owned spot is so popular early in the day that it's best to arrive late—between 9:30 and 10:30 A.M.—for a seat.

Breakfast may have been filling, but you and your honey have to plan ahead for lunch. Stop by the **Honeybaked Ham Company** (8608 Abercorn Street; 912–920–7400; inexpensive) and buy some delicious sweet ham sandwiches, cheese, fruit, and drinks for a picnic later in the day. Once you've packed your cooler, it's time to head out for a little batting practice.

The **Allen E. Paulson Softball Complex** (7171 Skidaway Road; 912–351–3852) has been noted as one of the grandest such facilities in this part of the country. During the spring and summer seasons, the fields here are abuzz with softball action as nearly 130 teams vie for church and coed league pennants. Call the stadium to get the lineup and plan to take in the action if the night air beckons. In fall as many as eighty teams participate on the five fully lighted fields.

The site of two national tournaments in 1997, the complex is also a special place for the two of you to go for some private practice in the batting cage, so venture over to the Skidaway Road entrance for a swingin' time. The balls are in the machine in the batting cage; when you put your money in, they shoot out. You should bring your own bat or purchase a used one from **Play It Again Sports** (1100 Eisenhower Drive, Eisenhower Square Shopping Center; 912–691–1855), a secondhand sporting equipment shop located about a mile from the batting cages.

From the softball complex, you're within walking distance of the **Paul Anderson–Howard Cohen Weightlifting Center** (7232 Varnedoe Drive; 912–351–3500), watch Olympic-style weight lifting and strength training in progress. One never knows which athletes will be there, so ask when you enter the facility. Often there are notable personalities (and previous world medal winners) to watch for in the next Olympics. The center is open to the public from 8:00 A.M. to 8:00 P.M. Monday through Friday; closed Sunday. If you're properly dressed for working out, feel free to try out the machines or check out your own strength. There is no admission fee, but users must sign a waiver to work out and equipment availability may be limited. The facility is home to Team Savannah, a world-renowned weight-lifting team filled with its own champions.

A few minutes' drive along a nearby stretch of road, will bring you to the **Chatham County Aquatic Center** (7240 Sallie Mood

Net a Gnat

*Savannahians have grown so accustomed to the relentlessness of pesky sand gnats that they have given up on temporary treasures like insect repellents. Instead, they purchase "gnat suits" consisting of a see-through, breathable net shirt with full head covering and pants that slide easily over shorts. The net suits allow air to flow through the fabric, but the holes are so small that they're impenetrable by the gnats. During the 1996 Summer Olympic Yachting Events held in Savannah, international sailors learned of the suits and purchased them from marine supply shops for protection. You can buy a set of suits from the **Sail Harbor Marina** (618 Wilmington Island Road, Wilmington Island; 912–897–2896) and test them out on the boardwalk of the marina's bar, **The Lightship Tavern.***

Drive; 912–351–6556). Go south on Abercorn to Eisenhower Drive. Proceed east on Eisenhower to Sallie Mood Drive, where you'll take a right. About a half mile down, the massive structure will be on your left. This state-of-the-art facility plays host to local, state, and national meets throughout the year, so ask for a schedule upon your arrival. The beautiful pool is open to the public from noon to 4:00 P.M. and 4:30 to 9:00 P.M. weekdays, 11:00 A.M. to 6:00 P.M. Saturday, and noon to 6:00 P.M. Sunday. Admission for a swim is $4.00 per person, so bring along bathing suits and try out the 50-meter pool together. Check the schedule for a list of upcoming meets, and if you're lucky enough to chance upon one in progress, stick around for the action.

DAY ONE: afternoon

Lake Mayer Community Park (Montgomery Crossroad and Sallie Mood Drive; 912–652–6786) is to Savannah what Central Park is to New York. To reach it from the Aquatic Center, drive about a mile and a half down Sallie Mood Drive. Turn left onto Montgomery Crossroad. Lake Mayer is clearly marked, about a quarter of a mile from the turnoff. Wildlife abounds in this natural setting, as do recreational opportunities of many kinds. The south side of the sprawling seventy-five acre park boasts a beautiful thirty-five acre lake surrounded by a 1.5-mile walking and jogging track that is accented with eighteen fitness stations. Eight lighted tennis courts, two basketball courts, and even a remote-control auto racetrack keep the park popping with almost nonstop action throughout the day. Plan ahead for an enjoyable afternoon here by bringing along the gear you might need to participate in your favorite activities. (Don't bring bathing suits; swimming is not permitted in the lake.) If you're "pole-less," stop by **Cranman's Sporting World** (401 East Montgomery Crossroad; 912–921–1488) for a cane pole ($4.00 to $5.00 per pole) and a bucket of worms. The crappie, catfish, and bream are always biting, but you have to have a freshwater fishing license. A one-day license costs $3.50 per person, and you can get them at Cranman's.

If you've always wanted to learn to sail, you're in the right place. Lake Mayer is host to the **Savannah Sailing Center** (at Lake Mayer; 912–231–9996), where courses are taught on-site at the boathouse. Rates are $80 for spring programs or $25 per session for adult sailors; call for reservations.

By late afternoon you two may need a time-out, if not a substitution. Head for your cool, modern room for check-in, a shower, and maybe even a nap at the popular **Hampton Inn Historic District** (201 East Bay Street; 912–231–9700; $139 to $149 king seasonal weekend rate). If you prefer newness to historic authenticity, you'll enjoy these spacious rooms. The decor reflects historic inns of Savannah with antique reproductions, wallpaper, and lighting. Hampton puts you right onto the sidewalk of Bay Street and directly across from Factor's Walk and River Street. Prices are lower than at most inns, and you're still provided with the modern conveniences of a fine hotel.

DAY ONE: evening

Popcorn and peanuts are the fare of the evening, so stash some dollar bills in your pocket and put on your best T-shirt and baseball cap. The Savannah Sand Gnats are in town, and if the film *Bull Durham* set your heart to pounding, picture Kevin Costner at the plate and cheer on the Gnats. The setting is Savannah's jewel of a baseball park, **Grayson Stadium** (1401 East Victory Drive; 912–351–9150), and the mascot is a giant sand gnat. Old-timers, babies, and hard-nosed baseball fans are sitting in these newly painted stands, and the redbrick stadium is filled with action at least two nights a week during summer (call ahead to request a schedule). If you purchase a pass for the Stadium Club, a sprawling wooden deck overlooking the park, you can sit at a table for two while you enjoy the action from above the field.

In 1904 several minor-league club owners gathered in Savannah at the old DeSoto Hilton to organize minor-league baseball in the South. The result was the SALLY League (South Atlantic League), and throughout the 1930s and 1940s the sport grew to phenomenal proportions. The 1947 Savannah Indians, along with star pitcher and minor-league legend Lou Brissie, drew crowds totaling 192,000. The Savannah minor-league baseball team has, through the years, changed ownership. Presently owned by the Texas Rangers, the "gnats" have become a favorite Savannah diversion for visitors and residents.

Seventy-one games are played each season at the stadium, which was built in 1941 and seats 5,000 (so don't worry about a sellout). Sip a cold beer and munch on boiled peanuts as you browse through the program, which offers a brief history of the team and its facilities. The Gnats were owned by the Los Angeles Dodgers; the 1998 season brought affiliation with the American League's Texas Rangers. The team captured the SALLY League championships in 1993, 1994, and 1996. If you buy a pack of Sand Gnats baseball cards, one day you could be holding on to something valuable: That minor leaguer you watched on your visit to Savannah could very well become a famous player.

Games start at 7:15 P.M. weekdays and at 2:00 P.M. on Saturday

A Heavenly Treat

Don your exercise duds and prepare to work up a sweat in the chic, contemporary **Downtown Athletic Club** (1 East Broughton Street; 912–236–4874; $7.00 guest fee for use of the facilities for a day). The toned glutes of Melanie Griffith, Demi Moore, Daryl Hannah, Clint Eastwood, and Heather Locklear have been here, as they dash in and out of Savannah during filming breaks, vacations, and short visits to the city. Club owner Alan Jennings and his wife, Ginger, can set you up for a relaxing massage for two. After you've showered, share fat-free treats and fruit drinks at the club's juice bar.

and Sunday. General admission is $5.00 for adults. You can park under the live oaks for free and generally experience a joyful evening beneath the stars for little cost or effort.

DINNER

Snuggle up to your sport and catch the latest scores at one of the great sports-bar "dives" in the South. **Coach's Corner** (3016 East Victory Drive in Thunderbolt; 912–352–2933; inexpensive) is the place to dine on sesame chicken fingers, hot onion rings, spicy fries, and all the junk food one indulges in when the urge strikes. Coach's is a place where you can sit close and cheer on Savannah's favorites, The Atlanta Braves; if you're in town for a fall visit, college football is the fare. There's nothing fancy about this little house that's been a Savannah institution for twenty-five years, and if you don't like sports, have no fear! You and your partner can test your intelligence playing Interactive Trivia against each other. Ask the waitress for two control panels, and as you dip your fries into the mound of ketchup you just poured, tickle your mate's brain cells with your trivia answers.

After dinner, drive east on Victory Drive about ½ mile, turning right onto River Drive. This is one of Savannah's most scenic streets. Drive all the way down the street until it ends at the parking lot of the River's End restaurant. Park your car and stroll down to the water-front, where the view of shrimp boats and yachts will provide a scenic diversion.

DAY TWO: morning

Arise as the city is coming alive and the traffic begins to move slowly along Bay Street. Before checking out of the hotel, enjoy the com-plimentary fresh fruit and pastries at the Hampton, then spend the remainder of your stay in the wilds at **Skidaway Island State Park** (52 Diamond Causeway; 912–598–2300; $2.00 per car). Twenty minutes from the Historic District, the park is a perfect getaway for adventurers. Take Abercorn Street to Mall Boulevard, turn left, then quickly right on Hodgson Memorial Drive, left on Montgomery Crossroad, then right on Whitefield Avenue east to the Diamond Causeway. The route takes you along salt marshes with sights of egrets, gulls, and sandpipers feeding. Fiddler crabs burrow in the mud, and anglers float lazily by in small fishing skiffs. The 533-acre state park is in the midst of a maritime forest and has interpretive trails and nature programs. Be sure to pick up a free map of the park and trails, and impress your mate by finding your way through the thick, woodsy area. You'll navigate through forest as well as salt marsh, passing Civil War fortifications and even a moonshine still in this hidden paradise. Then get back on the road to civilization.

FOR MORE ROMANCE

Contact **Sail Harbor Marina** (618 Wilmington Island Road; 912–897–2896) for a listing of sailing regattas hosted throughout the year by various local sailing clubs. The marina is located near the site of all the action, and you can sit on the dock as the competition begins. Enjoy the launching from an outdoor eatery called **The Lightship Tavern** (adjacent to the marina; 912–898–9182; inexpensive). Share a sandwich and cold drink from the deck overlooking the marina and marsh.

Another imaginative option for this itinerary is a trip to **Delta Plantation** (P.O. Box 1900, Hardeeville, SC; 912–398–1849; inexpensive to moderate), a five-minute drive from downtown Savannah across the Savannah River Bridge. Established in the late 1700s by rice farmer and war hero Langdon Chavis, the old home provided land for the Old Savannah highway used by George Washington in 1792. Delta prospered for many years until most of the property's Southern-style buildings were burned to the ground by General Sherman on his rampage in the South. After his attack on the plantation, he set up his headquarters nearby. Today, the 1,700 acres that were once rice fields harvested by more than 400 slaves echo with an overwhelming sense of history. Professional tour guides will lead you and your mate on a firsthand look at the abundant wildlife through a walking, horseback, kayak, or bus tour. Lowcountry lunch and dinner can be arranged on request, and the cost of each tour differs according to the type and number in the party.

Deap-sea fishing with your partner can be quite an adventurous thrill aboard any of the several seafaring vessels the area has to offer. From the Lazaretto Creek Pier at Tybee Island to the Bull River Marina, fishing charters are abundant in this area. Private charters from four to fifteen hours are available, and bait, tackle, rods, and reels are included. Fish cleaning is also available. Rates range from $125 to $500 for all-day trips. Call **Captain Ed** (912–897–1380), **Miss Judy** (912–897–4921), **Amick's Deep Sea Fishing, Inc.** (912–897–6759), or **Neva-Miss** (912–897–2706) for a fun-filled day on the high seas.

ITINERARY 18
Two days and one night

Love on Two Wheels
A Bicycling Weekend

S OME PEOPLE WHO LIVE IN SAVANNAH never drive cars. One of them is *Savannah News-Press* entertainment writer Gene Downs, who would rather weave through downtown traffic on a bike than sit in it bumper to bumper. Gene swears that biking is the best and most romantic way to see the city. At street level you can be face to face with history and delighted by the colors of the buildings and parks. This weekend you're a team with a mission—to see the city in all its glory, sharing in the ecstasy on a pair of bikes. Either way, hang on for a romantic ride through the streets of Savannah.

PRACTICAL NOTES: If a sudden downpour threatens this mainly outdoor weekend, take shelter in a River Street pub, an old museum fort, or a quaint boutique. Savannah is made for showers, so when in Savannah, do as the natives do: Enjoy it.

Bring along plenty of extra drinking water and good bicycle locks. Call The Bicycle Link to rent your bikes of choice. Then take a deep breath and follow these tips from Gene Downs:

- A bike is considered a vehicle, so observe all traffic signals and signs as if you were driving.

- Stay as close to the right-hand side of the road as possible.

- Cross bumpy railroad tracks or uneven streets at right angles and walk your bike across dangerous intersections.

- Don't argue back if Savannahians, who aren't too friendly toward bikers, honk their horns or threaten. Stay calm and maneuver carefully. The sights you see will be well worth the aggravation of putting up with impatient drivers.

Romance AT A GLANCE

◆ Start your trek on two wheels at **The Bicycle Link** (22 West Broughton Street; 912–233–9401) where you and your loved one can rent bikes to savor the city at eye level.

◆ Pick up lunch at **Roly Poly** (114 Barnard Street; 912–233–8222), an extraordinary sandwich shop, and share a sandwich in the square.

◆ Dine in one of the most romantic restaurants within miles, **Hunter House Inn** (1701 Butler Avenue, Tybee Island; 912–786–7515).

◆ Sleep under the stars at the **River's End Campground** (just off Highway 80 East; 912–786–5518).

◆ Cruise the beach on your bike at low tide and explore the beautiful **Fort Screven** area of Tybee, where officer's quarters are now restored beach homes. Circle the island, marveling at the wildlife you'll see off the way.

◆ Stop by the **Tybee Island Lighthouse** (30 Meddin Drive; 912–786–5801) and climb it for a view that will be the perfect backdrop for your self-made postcard.

◆ Dance to reggae music on the patio or sample the plantains at the **North Beach Grill** (41A Meddin Drive; 912–786–9003).

DAY ONE: afternoon

Get yourselves in gear and head over to **The Bicycle Link** (22 West Broughton Street; 912–233–9401; hours from 10:00 A.M. to 6:00 P.M. Monday through Saturday) to rent a pair of bikes.

LUNCH

Ride east on West Broad to Barnard and proceed north to a unique downtown eatery, **Roly Poly** (114 Barnard Street; 912–233–8222; inexpensive), where you can order from a variety of more than fifty freshly made rolled sandwiches, including Sante Fe Chicken (sliced chicken breast, jalapeño cheese, onions, tomatoes, and dressing with a side of salsa) or a low-fat oriental chicken roll-up (low-fat chicken breast, lettuce, tomato, sprouts, cucumber, carrots, green pepper, mango chutney, and sesame dressing). The tiny eatery is located just off State Street, with beautiful Telfair Square to its left.

Purchase your sandwiches, lock up your bikes, and choose a bench in the square where you can sit and dine.

After you have shared your lunch on **Telfair Square,** follow Barnard Street, where you'll find the beautiful Telfair mansion (now an art museum; see pages 17–18). Follow Barnard until it intersects with Oglethorpe and then turn left onto Oglethorpe and ride until you reach Whitaker Street. Stop here to admire the **Independent Presbyterian Church.** President Woodrow Wilson married a Savannahian (to her family's dismay) here.

Ride from Whitaker Street to Bull Street and head toward the riverfront. You'll circle a variety of squares, and you'll pass **Chippewa Square**, the site of fictional character Forrest Gump's saga. (His bench is not here; it was only a Hollywood prop, but if you have seen the film you'll recognize the square even without it.) Next, take a spin around **Forsyth Park** (but don't ride in the park itself). You may bike around the park starting at the corner of Gaston and Whitaker Streets. When you reach Broughton Street, take a right and cycle past new businesses, restaurants, and shops that have been restored recently.

Return your bike to the shop and refresh yourselves with a long, cool drink of water, then leave Savannah by car and head to the beach.

Your Nose Knows

The salty sea breeze of Tybee Island will refresh you and your companion as you journey toward the ocean down the palm-lined, two-lane Tybee Road (U.S. Highway 80 East). The early Native American inhabitants named the island Tybee, meaning "salt." To those who are strangers to the coast, the scent of salt air may be unfamiliar, but some say it's a natural aphrodisiac. Let it work its magic on the two of you—it can't hurt to breathe deeply.

DAY ONE: evening

Check into **River's End Campground** (just off Highway 80 East at Tybee Island; 912–786–5518; $20 to $30 per night for RV camping, $8.00 per night for tent camping, and $99 to $109 per night for fully furnished, one-bedroom cottages). Completely shaded and within steps of the sand, this is a delightful place to stay. It is best to call ahead for reservations as this has become a popular site. The staff is friendly, however, and the rest rooms are clean. If you choose to reserve your bike for tomorrow now, try calling the **Pack Rat Bicycle Shop** (1405 Butler Avenue, Tybee Island; 912–786–4013). Rates are $10 a day. The shop is open 10:00 A.M. to 6:00 P.M.; closed on Tuesday.

DINNER

You've earned an evening out. Dine at **The Hunter House Inn** (1701 Butler Avenue; Tybee Island; 912–786–7515; expensive), where you can kick back after dinner and rest on the front porch in gigantic rockers. As with all Tybee restaurants, the attire here is casual. The charm of this inn is what you need to pamper yourselves before a day of roughing it. Candlelit tables with fresh flowers, cozy dining rooms that seat only a few at a time, and a sumptuous menu will be tempting after your afternoon jaunt. Order a cup of creamy tomato cognac seafood bisque and the grilled grouper or a hearty steak. Meals come with homemade bread, so there's hardly room for dessert. Besides, the great outdoors is calling. Return to your campsite and crawl into your double sleeping bag for a sound and refreshing snooze that will reenergize you for your morning ride around the island.

DAY TWO: morning

BREAKFAST

Put a knapsack on one of the pair of you and fill it with a picnic blanket and snacks, then spend today biking around Tybee Island. Try the **Sunrise Restaurant** (1511 Butler Avenue; 912–786–7473; inexpensive). Their "hash brown deluxe," a mixture of fresh broccoli, onions, ham, and potatoes, is super.

Climb aboard your bikes and cycle down Sixteenth Street for a taste of nostalgia. You'll pass tiny eateries and rustic pubs. Cruise the oceanside and circle back to Butler Avenue, Tybee's main drag.

Head down Butler, stopping on any numbered street to your right if you'd like to take a quick look at the ocean. Your "quick

Dive on Legs——
Crab Legs, That Is

*Swaying palm trees frame the billowing marsh grasses, and your waterside table at **Snapper's Seafood Restaurant** (104 Bryan Woods Road; 912–897–6101; moderate) is the perfect setting for a steamy evening. Order a bucket-to-share of steamed snow-crab legs. For the sensual task of devouring your treat, your server will provide the necessary tools: a pair of nutcrackers and warm, melted butter for saturating the sweet crabmeat. Choose a blush-colored limb, crack the hard shell, peel it back, dip the exposed meat in butter, and bring the curvy leg right to your your lips. Suck this divine Southern delicacy out of its hull and reach for the next leg. Sublime. When you have finished this spirited ritual, cleanse and soften your hands with the fragrant wiping cloths brought to your table, and slip away for more romance in the evening ahead.*

look" might just turn into several hours if you choose to venture over the walkways and onto the beach. In fact, do just that! Skim the beach on your bike—the views of the ocean and sunbathers are equally eye-catching! The sand is hard and perfect for bike riding, especially at low tide. Exit at the **Beachside Colony** (404 Butler Avenue; 913–786–4535), where you can sip daiquiris with locals in the oceanside lounge. Get back on track now—you've been distracted!

You'll spot the Tybee Lighthouse straight ahead, but first take a right onto Second Avenue (just after you reach the sharp curve on Butler) and enter the **Fort Screven** area. Here you'll see stately, Southern, two-story, white clapboard houses with wide front porches filled with wicker furniture, flourishing ferns, and ocean breezes. These beautiful homes served as officers' quarters from the time of the Spanish-American War to the conclusion of World War II. A beautiful park is on your left. If you have any spare trail mix or crackers in your knapsack, you can stop and feed the ducks.

When Cedarwood Drive turns into Meddin, you're almost to the historic **Tybee Lighthouse** (30 Meddin Drive; 912–786–5801). Park here and feel your heart rate climb as you walk to the top of the tower. If you race your partner, you may fall exhausted into each other's arms when you reach the panoramic observation area 150-plus feet above the sand. The view extends for 18 miles. Pat yourselves on the back! This is the tallest lighthouse in Georgia, and you're sittin' on top o' the state.

DAY TWO: afternoon

LUNCH

The reggae music from **North Beach Grill** (41A Meddin Drive; 912-786-9003; inexpensive) is begging you to stop for a cold drink and a delicious crab burger. No need to wear your shoes. Kick them off and sit outside on the shaded deck as the ocean breezes cool you off.

It's difficult to leave this favorite hangout, but duty calls! Ride on around Meddin Drive until you reach Van Horn. Follow it until you see the campground and take a right (no naps just yet). Ride all the way down and head left until you reach Highway 80 East. Pedal hard and proceed over the Lazaretto Creek Bridge and you'll soon come to historic **Fort Pulaski.** Turn right and ride into the fort. Park your bike and lock it up in the racks provided (bikes are not permitted inside the fort).

Once inside, playfully weave in and out of the notable archways of this fortress where Robert E. Lee was assigned duty after graduating from the U.S. Military Academy at West Point. A moat still exists around the fort, and you'll see evidence of the destruction that occurred during the Civil War.

Spread your blanket on the designated picnic areas on this island called Cockspur. Replenish your liquids, rest, and then head across Highway 80 to the public dock at Lazaretto Creek. The sun is beginning to set, and the dolphins are getting playful as the shrimp boats chug into the marina. Absorb the beauty of this place before climbing back on your bike and pedaling across the bridge to your final destination, **Cafe Loco** (1 Highway 80 East; 912-786-7810; inexpensive). Jimmy Buffet music is playing, so venture out onto the waterside dock. Before it gets dark, pedal back to the Pack Rat bike shop and turn your bikes in. Take one last look around before you leave; the sun is setting and the lights of Savannah are shining in the distance.

The Rules

*As an alternative to visiting Fort Pulaski, why not try a totally different kind of adventure—crabbing! Stop at the **Tybee Market IGA** (1111 Butler Avenue; 912–786–4601) and purchase a raw chicken neck, some kite string, a small cooler, some ice, and a crab net. Sound romantic? Not quite. But if you're never tried your hand at crabbing, you'll discover a diversion that's not only challenging but rewarding—especially if you lure a big one. Bike to the back side of the island to the small creek just around the corner from the campground on Polk Avenue. Then follow these time-tested rules: Tie your chicken neck to the string and toss it out into the creek. Pull the string in slowly until you can barely see through the water and, if you've been lucky enough to attract a crab, net it! If you're not planning to cook and eat the creature, kindly toss it back into the creek for someone else to catch.*

For More Romance

From Tybee Island, bike back down Highway 80 heading into town. Your safety will be taken care of when you reach the **Tybee Island Rails-to-Trails** bike path, created to provide cyclists with their own lanes and special amenities for cruising down busy Highway 80. Along the way are picnic-table rest stops, and in the salt marshes alongside the path you'll see turtles, gulls, and egrets, as well as other spectators. The trek is magnificent! But be forewarned: This trip is for hard-core bikers only.

Touching Toes
A Fitness Retreat in Hilton Head

HAT HAPPENS WHEN A COUPLE loses weight together? According to marketing director Laura Cannavo at the plush **Hilton Head Health Institute** (14 Valencia Road, Hilton Head Island, S.C.; 843–785–7292), "When the body image is better, people feel better about their bodies and their life begins to change. They dress sexier and have more energy." So if the two of you think you could use a little physical toning, why not do it in tandem? You'll find that clean, fresh air, the steam from a sauna, and massage therapy for two can be the best aphrodisiacs. Pack your athletic gear and prepare to be transformed. After your stay here, especially if it's for a week or two, you're going to feel better, act better, and dive head-first into a sea of love and health.

PRACTICAL NOTES: The Hilton Head Health Institute encourages its guests to bring plenty of exercise attire, a good pair of sneakers for walking or biking, sunscreen, bug spray, and patience. Call them for information on rates or to make your reservation. Retreats are tailored to your needs and schedule.

A TYPICAL DAY: morning

When you arrive, you'll check into a beautiful, fully furnished "beachy," villa with bowls of complimentary fresh fruit and fresh vases of flowers (order prior to your arrival). Your first day begins at 7:00 A.M., and a fun, energetic, and romantic schedule follows for both of you.

◆ Get physical with your mate at the **Hilton Head Health Institute** (14 Valencia Road, Hilton Head Island; 843–785–7292).

◆ Savor every morsel as you dine five times a day with your mate at your side.

◆ Walk together around the lush grounds, finding solitude and relaxation while getting in shape.

◆ Indulge in a side-by-side massage in your villa.

BREAKFAST

The diet you'll begin consists of eating five times a day. The three main meals are low-calorie, healthful offerings. The two mini- or metabo-meals consist of a nutritious snack such as cereal or a piece of fruit.

Following breakfast, you and your mate will exercise, a regimen you'll repeat each time after eating. Next comes a thirty-minute "thermal walk"—that is, a workout moderately paced to boost your metabolic rate by 20 to 25 percent for the next three hours. No touching here—you need to swing your arms when you walk to burn calories more quickly. The beautiful grounds are shaded with live oaks and tall pines. Pick your preferred locations. You'll pass sleeping alligators, wild egrets, and other marsh wildlife and enjoy the serenity of the island while spending time with your companion.

A TYPICAL DAY: afternoon

LUNCH

Share lunch with your love privately in your villa, or, if you choose, in a recently remodeled dining room. If you dine on the deck of your villa, be prepared for guests that may include blue jays, chickadees, or squirrels. Fresh flowers will adorn your outdoor table, and the silence will be breathtaking.

After your healthful meal, take another walk around the tranquil grounds before heading, hand in hand, to an inspirational meeting. Your energetic leader makes certain that these educational seminars and group therapy sessions are fun, filled with humorous illustrations and creative ways to burn fat! Your leader encourages self-evaluation first, transforming couples who are unhappy with being overweight to feeling better, perhaps younger, and kicking up their heels with new activities. Meeting rooms overlook lagoons and golf courses. Groups include about twenty participants per session.

Each day's schedule differs and offers a combination of strength training, aerobic exercise, and therapy sessions. You'll also have anywhere from one to several hours of free time daily. Nearby amenities on the island include 12 miles of white sandy beaches; horseback riding; golf and tennis courses; sea kayaking, fishing, and sailing; music, theater, and movies; and loads of shopping. The institute will assist you in arranging a golf game and will provide you with transportation to your destination, if you desire.

After these active pursuits, you might want to indulge in a massage before dinner, given by one of the institute's licensed therapists. Share this relaxing experience together in the privacy of your own villa.

Provocative Preparations

Sign up for a cooking class for two at the Hilton Head Health Institute. Feeding the fresh ingredients to your mate as you prepare healthy menu items is one way to charge up your mealtime and make you forget all about the word diet.

A TYPICAL DAY: evening

DINNER

A romantic dinner for two consisting of baked or grilled chicken or fish, nutritious tasty salads, and grilled vegetables will be served by candlelight in the main dining room. Don't worry about overeating. It won't happen. Take a thirty-minute after-dinner walk together on the beach at sunset before heading back to the main auditorium for another inspirational meeting. Then stroll by the light of the moon—arms around those thinner waists—back to your villa for some quiet time.

FOR MORE ROMANCE

Get tickled after your day at the spa! **Coconuts Comedy Night Club** (15 Heritage Plaza; 843–686–6887; inexpensive) on Hilton Head Island is a small club featuring nationally known comedians Wednesday through Saturday at 9:30 P.M. (A nonsmoking show is held on Thursday at 9:30 P.M.) The club offers a full bar and light snack menu, and dress is casual. Admission is $10 per person.

Tee for Two

A GOLF GETAWAY IN HILTON HEAD

HE PRISTINE GREENS OF HILTON HEAD ISLAND golf courses glisten in the morning sun. Through the woods surrounding these lush courses, wild deer roam and graceful egrets tiptoe about. There's a certain serenity in experiencing a golf course—even during a tournament when appreciative fans gathered around a green cheer after a pro makes a shot. Watching golf requires a respect for silence. Despite the action on the fairways, you can still hear the birds chatter through the trees and watch the alligators lie still along the banks in the sun. For this itinerary, let your eyes and expressions do the talking.

PRACTICAL NOTES: This itinerary is designed for those who play golf, those who watch golf, and those who do neither. Wear comfortable, rubber-soled shoes (no spikes at Harbour Town). Wear golf attire and bring along plenty of sunscreen. Make your reservations well in advance of MCI Classic weekend in April and purchase tickets and badges by phone (800–234–1107) early. Practice-round badges are $30, and if you'd like to participate in the excitement of the full tournament, purchase your badge prior to February 2 for $90 (it's $100 after that date).

DAY ONE: afternoon

Check into the room you've reserved at the **Hyatt Regency Hilton Head Resort** (1 Hyatt Circle, Hilton Head; 800–233–1234 or 843–785–1234; $175 to $320) at Oceanfront Palmetto Dunes. You'll discover that everything you need for your stay on the island

*R*om*a*nce
AT A GLANCE

♦ Join the throngs of golf lovers at the **MCI Classic,** one of South Carolina's most blessed events played on the most picturesque golf course in the country!

♦ Check into the **Hyatt Regency Hilton Head** (Hyatt Circle, Hilton Head Island; 843-233-1234) along with the golf celebrities and head for the poolside bar where the crowds gather at sunset.

♦ Brush up on your game at **Pirate's Island Adventure Golf** (8 Marina Side Drive; 843-686-4001), then head to dinner at **Hemingway's at the Hyatt** (843-785-1234) where the treasures of the sea are prepared to your liking.

♦ Hit **Harbour Town** as the golf action gets under way and head toward the eighteenth hole where the yachts are gathering.

is right on site: poolside bars for daiquiri-sipping evenings, a fine romantic restaurant with a magnificent view of the Atlantic Ocean, and even a small grocery store. The ten-story hotel is one of the grandest on the East Coast as well as one of the largest. Even with 505 guest rooms, the size of the resort doesn't interfere with your opportunities to be alone together. The luxurious rooms are cheerfully decorated in pastel-colored linens, and many face the ocean. Reserve one of these, and you'll enjoy the majestic view from your private balcony.

LUNCH

When you have unpacked your things and refreshed yourselves after your drive, stop by the **Possum Point** poolside restaurant at the hotel for a light salad. Sit at one of the outside tables under a brightly colored umbrella and enjoy the magnificent view of the Atlantic Ocean.

After lunch, "cut loose," as they say in the South, and have some fun at **Pirate's Island Adventure Golf** (8 Marina Side Drive; 843-686-4001). This miniature golf course, a visual winner in a recent miniature golf competition, is full of challenging holes. Waterfalls and other obstacles make your play exciting and treacherous. The relaxed pace will give you an opportunity to brush up on your putting, the serious part of the game.

When you leave these greens, spend some time in the shops at **Shelter Cove Harbour** (William Hilton Parkway), a Mediterranean-like village anchored by huge yachts at a connecting marina. Everything from fine jewelry to T-shirts is sold along this waterfront mall.

DAY ONE: evening
DINNER

One of Hilton Head's most romantic dining establishments is located right in your hotel. You'll think you're in Key West when you enter **Hemingway's** (843-785-1234; expensive), the oceanfront restaurant and lounge named for the writer. Hemingway's features the "treasures" of the sea, including charbroiled or blackened grouper, swordfish, tuna, mahimahi, red snapper, or sea bass. Maryland-style crab cakes are superb lump crabmeat tossed in fresh herbs, baked, and served with a lemon caper remoulade. Filet mignon will please meat lovers. Save room for a sublime slice of the Grand Marnier cheesecake—ask for two forks and share.

DAY TWO: morning
BREAKFAST

Rise early and take a walk on the beach before enjoying a full breakfast at the hotel's cafe, which opens at 6:30 A.M. The garden-view eatery features a wonderful breakfast buffet for $11.50 per person and even offers a lighter version of the same menu for $5.75 per person. Enjoy nearly any breakfast item imaginable (sausage, bacon, ham, toast, eggs, omelettes, waffles, grits) before checking out of the hotel and making your way to the excitement of professional golf.

DAY TWO: afternoon

A shuttle will whisk you away to **Harbour Town,** where you'll be dropped off at another location to await a bus that will take you to the tournament. The bright greens of the manicured lawns, the pinks, yellows, and reds of the floral-designed entranceway, and the mass of color from the spectators are a sight to behold. The

Harbour Town Golf Links is one of the most beautiful courses in the country. The bus will drop you off amid the splendor of massive yachts that encircle the harbor, and you'll follow signs to the tournament entrance. You'll land near the first tee, where you can find a leader board and follow the list of golfers coming up to the first green. More than a hundred players are invited yearly, and most are coming off a week of play at The Masters tournament in nearby Augusta. In the four full days of golf, players compete for $1.5 million in prize money. Pick your favorite player to follow throughout the day.

LUNCH

Scattered along the course are vendors selling everything from barbecue sandwiches to chocolate-covered ice cream treats. Find a tree stump to sit and rest upon as you share a meal; at times like these, you may even forget there's a tournament going on.

Follow the map of the greens and make your way over to the eighteenth hole, situated at the edge of the Atlantic Ocean. The sun will likely be shining brightly, and a caravan of boats will be bobbing alongside the shoreline. Find a patch of dry grass and sit for the remainder of the day, applauding as each golfer finishes the play.

DAY TWO: evening

DINNER

At the close of the day on the links, walk around the marina to the **Quarterdeck** (Harbour Town, Hilton Head; 843–671–2222; expensive), the best place to watch the sun set on the island. If seafood is your fare of choice, they will cook it to your liking. The steaks are fabulous too.

After dinner, lounge in rockers scattered about the quaint shopping area. If you are sunburned and a bit weary, call the hotel shuttle to pick you up and whisk you back to the hotel. Return to your car and say goodbye to this tropical paradise in the Old South.

FOR MORE ROMANCE

Rose Hill Plantation (Highway 278; 843–757–2160) is one of the most picturesque semiprivate courses near Hilton Head Island (public playing is still available). Located on the mainland side, it has twenty-seven holes with par at seventy-two. The course is in close proximity to the end of the island, and when you finish nine holes (eighteen if you have time before dark), it'll be easy to hit the interstate or the road back to Savannah—a twenty-minute drive in which crossing the expansive Savannah River Bridge at sunset will be a highlight of your day.

Port City Potpourri II

A SCAD of Romance

THE SAVANNAH COLLEGE OF ART AND DESIGN

HE SAVANNAH COLLEGE OF ART AND DESIGN (SCAD) has created a core of more than fifty romantic buildings that have been restored in recent years, and the college's status as the largest art school in the world is bringing in talent from all over the globe. Visually stimulating buildings have bred unique restaurants, and beautiful outdoor gardens and the college's galleries showcase one-of-a-kind paintings, sculpture, and computer images. Your visit to these facilities might just prompt you to enroll in an arts program yourselves when you return home.

PRACTICAL NOTES: Bring cash for purchasing artwork by undiscovered talents. Comfortable walking shoes are recommended. Make room reservations in advance at the Eliza Thompson House.

DAY ONE: morning

This art-filled itinerary can begin in the morning any weekday or on a Saturday morning or Sunday afternoon. The **Savannah College of Art and Design** (912–525–5225) holds what must surely be a record in historic preservation. The college has in recent years grown to occupy more than 1 million square feet in nearly fifty buildings scattered throughout the Historic District. Students majoring in architecture, art, or graphic design are encouraged to apply their learning to building design and restoration, thus contributing their

Rom**ance**
AT A GLANCE

♦ *Stay in the **Eliza Thompson House** (5 West Jones Street; 912–236–3620), an enchanting inn that's painted with Spanish moss and dark brick and filled with charm, where shades of pastels calm your nerves and a lush garden courtyard offers respite for you and your mate.*

♦ *Explore the architectural marvels created by the **Savannah College of Art and Design** (912–525–5225). You and your mate are about to discover the beauty of more than thirty restored buildings in downtown Savannah as you visit such sites as the **West Bank Galleries** (322 Martin Luther King Jr. Boulevard) and the **Pei Ling Chan Garden for the Arts** (adjacent to the West Bank). The school offers a complete listing of galleries.*

♦ *Dine in an artistic eatery, **The Tuscon Grill** (113 West Broughton Street; 912–233–9669), and ask for the booth in the back corner so you and your companion can watch the crowd flow in and out of this popular place for art students.*

own creativity to the continued development of the school. There are 112 on-campus galleries, which feature rotating displays. Gallery hours are 8:30 A.M. to 5:30 P.M. Monday through Friday, 10:00 A.M. to 4:00 P.M. Saturday, and 1:00 to 4:00 P.M. Sunday.

BREAKFAST

Have a healthy breakfast before you begin touring the various exhibition halls and galleries. Art school students adore **Brighter Day Natural Foods** (1102 Bull Street; 912–236–4703; inexpensive), a natural and organic food store with a juice bar and deli located at the south end of Forsyth Park (at the corner of Bull Street and Park Avenue). Try some fresh-fruit smoothies made with frozen strawberries, bananas, yogurt, and a hint of apple juice, or their freshly made muffins. Tables out along the sidewalk allow you to enjoy breakfast alfresco if the weather is nice.

Your first stop on a SCAD tour should probably be the **Pinnacle Gallery** (912–525–4950), at the corner of Liberty and Habersham Streets, which offers complete listings and brochures regarding all public SCAD galleries and is owned by the Savannah College of Art and Design. Recent exhibits at Pinnacle have included the works of Andy Warhol and, believe it or not, Tony Bennett, who visited the school as a guest artist.

The gallery shares a building with **Casey House** (318 East Liberty Street). Built in 1896, this former neighborhood confectionery was recently transformed into the college's B&B. The facility contains 10,800 square feet of redbrick balconies, six bedroom suites with full baths, a full kitchen, two parlor rooms, and a dining room. Although the B&B is not for the general public, the home is worth stopping at and admiring.

Next, walk over to 101 Martin Luther King Jr. Boulevard and peek into **Bergen Hall,** a building that was once an eyesore but now contains the photography department and three art galleries, primarily of photographic work. Designed by Cletus Bergen, the 41,950-square-foot structure features large industrial sash windows, exposed timber, interior brick walls, and ornamental cast-stone detail. In the 1980s Savannah architect and former SCAD student Barry Rentzel started the renovation for use as an office complex. The design is breathtaking and, when you enter the building, you'll be overwhelmed by an impressive five-story atrium shell. Peruse the galleries and stock up on film in the building's supply store.

LUNCH

Dine nearby in a unique SCAD eatery now so popular that you have to check the time (either before or well after the noon lunch hour) to get in the door. The **Gryphon Tea Room** (337 Bull Street; 912–525–5880; inexpensive), housed in a century-old pharmacy, is the perfect place to cool off and enjoy a light lunch. Tiffany-style globes hang above the tables, and lovely stained-glass windows have mortar-and-pestle motifs remaining from the drugstore days. Select a table near the window overlooking the square. For dessert order the plateful of scones, presented on antique china.

DAY ONE: afternoon

After lunch, visit **Poetter Hall and Library** (342 Bull Street), which was built in 1892 and designed to serve as the armory for the Savannah Volunteer Guards. The Romanesque Revival building features deep arches, massive corner towers, and ornate wrought-iron balconies that overlook Savannah's squares. The structure, which originally combined a drill hall, a large company room, a billiard room, and a club for the guards, is now a classroom building that also houses a graphic design studio and art departments. A skylit, ornate wooden staircase leads up to the library, which was once a ballroom.

West Bank Galleries (322 Martin Luther King Jr. Boulevard) is a standout and not to be missed. This former Savannah bank features contemporary, cutting-edge artwork. Recent shows have included the world premiere of a new work by video artist Bill Viola, an interactive exhibit by Japanese artist Masaki Fuhihata, and the introduction of "Leonardo da Vinci," a CD-ROM developed by Bill Gates's Cobras Corporation.

Your tour will end in the **Pei Ling Chan Garden for the Arts,** adjacent to the West Bank Gallery, a melting pot of international influences. The garden includes African-American, Asian, English, and French sections, as well as an amphitheater that hosts live performances and local events.

DAY ONE: evening

Check in at the **Eliza Thompson House** (5 West Jones Street; 800–348–9378; $105 to $230), which offers one of Savannah's few B&B rooms that costs around $100. Decorated in soothing shades of pink, blue, and green, this room, located at the front of the inn, is furnished in period antiques with a washstand and beautiful four-poster bed. It's called the Savannah Room, and it's a great deal at an inn that boasts one of the best reputations in the city. You can also opt for their most romantic—and most expensive—room. The purple-and-cream-colored Jay Stephen Room has a king-size four-poster canopy bed and a Jacuzzi and is yours for $230 per night. Unpack your bags, then bring this creative day to a close over dinner.

DINNER

Dine in the lively **Tuscon Grill** (113 West Broughton Street; 912–233–9669; inexpensive), an ethnic restaurant that is fast becoming a favorite for visitors seeking a cool, cozy place to celebrate the day's end. If you think that Savannah is not the place for American Southwestern cuisine, think again! This eatery offers a refreshing alternative to Savannah icons like Mrs. Wilkes and Elizabeth. A tiled entryway holds a cozy waiting area, Native American fetishes adorn the walls, and booths are dimly lit. Meals arrive with complimentary homemade nachos and two kinds of salsa. For entrees, choose coconut chile crusted tuna served with plantain fries, or try Jose's hash, made with fresh poached salmon served over black beans.

Afterward stroll down Broughton Street and take a right on Drayton. Then walk down to Jones Street, turn right, and you'll be at your B&B.

Hide-and-Seek

Play hide-and-seek, your favorite childhood game, in **Ex Libris** *(228 Martin Luther King Jr. Boulevard; 912–525–7550), a Savannah College of Art and Design building that now houses a coffee shop and bookstore. The facility boasts an industrial design, with wide-open interior spaces, massive wood beams, and an open stairwell. You can easily get lost amid the beauty of its 24,060 square feet. While your mate is browsing, purchase a sweet treat from the coffee shop and present it when you've found each other once again.*

DAY TWO: morning

Before leaving Eliza Thompson's, enjoy a full home-cooked breakfast in the outdoor courtyard. You'll be able to smell the freshly brewed coffee, the mouth-watering pastries, and the country ham from your room. Place your order in the main dining room; then, if the weather permits, select a bench or table from which you can enjoy a sumptuous Southern breakfast.

For more romance

Attend the Savannah College of Art and Design's **Student Sidewalk Arts Festival** held annually on the fourth Saturday in April. The site is Savannah's beautiful Forsyth Park. Students create elaborate drawings on the uneven sidewalks and pray that the weather cooperates. Musical entertainment is provided throughout the afternoon and occasionally into the night. Admission is free. For more information contact the school's community relations department at (912) 525-5225.

The college also sponsors an event each fall that is worth a trip to Savannah. You and your mate can snuggle for an entire week in the school's newly restored movie house, **Trustees Theater** (206 Broughton Street; 912-525-5050) for the Savannah Film and Video Festival. Celebrities often attend the festival, which is held the first week in November. It includes a weeklong lineup of old and new releases—professional and amateur—that range from two-minute shorts to full-length films. Prices for the festival range from year to year; call (912) 525-5225 for more information.

Something to Talk About
STEAMY SAVANNAH DETOURS

WHEN GRACE (JULIA ROBERTS) rounded the corner at historic Johnson Square and spied her husband, Eddie (Dennis Quaid), cheek to cheek with another woman, Savannah became the perfect setting for a second Civil War of sorts. Unfolding on the big screen was the tale of a couple torn apart by infidelity, seeking to light the fire once again in their marriage. The fire could have been lit anywhere, but Hollywood, a frequent visitor, had returned to the film *Something to Talk About* in the city where sets are ready-made.

There's no better place to observe the many faces of Savannah than on the big screen. It's a fact! When it comes to romance at its finest, Hollywood is in love with Savannah. You'll soon discover why Robert Redford chose the city for filming *The Legend of Bagger Vance*, a story set in Savannah in the 1920s and filmed in its entirety on the streets of this city. The city also played herself when Sandra Bullock and Ben Affleck lived in the steam of the summer filming *Forces of Nature*. To date, Savannah has more than thirty movie titles to her name. Now you'll be the stars of this set that heats up the big screen.

PRACTICAL NOTES: Rent some videos filmed in Savannah to better acquaint yourself with the city. Start with *Forrest Gump*, then wrap your arms around your mate and get in the mood with *Forces of Nature*. Bring along a camera and shoot the landmarks you've shared at home on TV.

♦ Bring the big screen close to your heart with this trip to Savannah. Shop the quaint boutiques in the streets of this city that were recently transformed into a scene right out of the 1920s for Robert Redford's The Legend of Bagger Vance.

♦ After you've covered the area around the City Market, buy your loved one a present at the place where all art culminates: the **Arts and Crafts Emporium** (234 Bull Street; 912–238–0003).

♦ Have lunch at the **Six Pence Pub** (245 Bull Street; 912–233–3156) where Julia Roberts came to blows with on-screen hubby Dennis Quaid in the film Something to Talk About.

♦ Get closer in a suite at the **Hilton Savannah DeSoto** (15 East Liberty Street; 912–232–9000), a grand hotel in the style Hollywood loves best.

♦ Star sightings are frequent in the hotel lobby, so keep your autograph book handy as you enjoy drinks in the **Lion's Den** (right inside the hotel) and dine at the **Magnolia Restaurant.**

DAY ONE: morning

BREAKFAST

Come to Savannah early and begin your adventures at one of Savannah's most popular morning gathering spots. **The Express Cafe** (39 Barnard Street; 912–233–4683; inexpensive) is a sunlit and enticing place to start your day. The aroma of freshly baking bread mingles with the fragrances of fresh muffins, pastries, fruit, and gourmet coffees. Stop just outside the cafe for a morning newspaper, then spend the first hour of your day in a captivating environment frequented by businesspeople, tourists, and students from the Savannah College of Art and Design. Feast on an assortment of these, or, if you're extra hungry, try a fluffy omelette filled with fresh vegetables.

At 10:00 A.M., leave the cafe in time for the opening of **Charles Leonard's** (33 Barnard Street; 912–238–4351) studio and shop next door to the cafe. Leonard has made a small fortune with his lithographs of sealife. Fabulous depictions of blue crabs, flounder, and red snapper adorn his walls and are for sale. After you've purchased

the catch of the day, venture into the **Kitchen Kaboodle** (31 Barnard Street; 912–238–3474), a Savannah favorite for fine kitchen cookware, French copperware, wine racks, bar accessories, and unique kitchen gift sets. Once you've treated yourselves to something fun, cross the street and visit **Terra Cotta** (34 Barnard Street; 912–236–6150), a luxurious, sensual store filled with fluffy bath apparel and quality bedclothes. Then browse the **Ray Ellis/Compass Prints** (205 West Congress Street; 912–234–3537) filled with Low Country images by artist Ray Ellis. Prints are available, as are original paintings (for a high price). For a less expensive memento of your trip, purchase one of the books of the artist's work. You'll find marsh scenes in soft greens, sailing scenes of nearby waters, and colorful images of Savannahians playing and socializing. The gallery is open from 10:00 A.M. to 4:00 P.M. Monday through Saturday.

DAY ONE: afternoon

From this tiny cluster of boutiques, cross over Whitaker Street into Johnson Square where, on Monday and Friday during the summer months, you'll be treated to live music starting at noon.

LUNCH

Follow Bull Street South to **Six Pence Pub** (245 Bull Street; 912–233–3156; inexpensive), the site of a Julia Roberts–Dennis Quaid encounter in *Something to Talk About*. (Imagine Julia peering through the outdoor windows and seeing her husband inside, partying with another woman.) This pub offers a delightful respite from the heat of the day, as the inside is dark and cool. Try the homemade potato salad and scrumptious sandwiches on home-baked bread (your choice of white, wheat, rye, or pumpernickel). On Friday and Saturday evenings live entertainment includes jazz, blues, and Irish folk music, and on any night the staff will be pleased to share stories of after-filming partying with the cast of the movie. Dennis Quaid, an accomplished pianist, reportedly played until the wee hours after one day of filming.

Just across the street is the **Arts and Crafts Emporium of Savannah** (234 Bull Street; 912–238–0003), where you can wander for hours through a maze of fascinating relics from craftspersons all over the country. The massive store holds old Savannah postcards, paintings, cookbooks, jewelry, and souvenirs galore.

Take the rest of the afternoon off (your feet) and enjoy a minibus architectural tour with **Gray Line of Historic Savannah** (215 West Boundary Street; 912–234–TOUR). Tours are one and a half hours long and range in price from $17 to $25.

DAY ONE: evening

Savannah's grand hotel, the **Hilton Savannah DeSoto** (15 East Liberty Street; 912–232–9000; $129 to $170 for standard rooms; $199 to $399 for suites, continues to reign as one of the city's most well-loved and popular hotels. As home to celebrities who visit for film or concert occasions, this beautiful hotel is freshly renovated and holds a special place in the hearts of Savannahians who have dined in its restaurants, socialized in its private club, and spent special occasions in its lavish suites.

Romance abounds in the pages of this historic hotel's history books. A festive New Year's Day society ball christened the hotel in 1890 and set the stage for years of energy and opulence. Characterized by its Romanesque architecture, the hotel has played host to more than five United States presidents. Celebrities such as Lady Astor, Margaret Mitchell, Lillian Russell, Gregory Peck, and Katherine Hepburn have sampled the hotel's luxurious rooms and suites in years past. The hotel's twelfth floor was recently converted to a Hilton Honors floor (king rooms with extra-long beds) which complements the thirteenth floor concierge level.

After you check in, take a refreshing swim in an outdoor heated pool for a refreshing respite from the city below. The view of Savannah's skyline from the deck is spectacular.

DINNER

Authentic Low Country cuisine is offered in the hotel's popular **Magnolia Restaurant** (912–232–9000; moderate).

Wrapped around all corners of the hotel are charming boutiques, quaint coffee shops, and fine restaurants, well within walking distance. When the stars beckon, visit lobby-side bar, **The Lion's Den,** for a nightcap before turning in. The bar features daily drink specials and live jazz on the weekends.

DAY TWO: morning

Awaken to a gorgeous Savannah morning and, like most Savannahians, head out for an early morning jog (or walk) in Forsyth Park. Your hotel sits at the corner of Bull Street, so head south on Bull and you'll run right into the park, only a couple of blocks away. Celebrity sightings are frequent, especially during movie-making times. Robert Redford, Demi Moore, Ben Affleck, Sandra Bullock, Kevin Spacey, Matt Damon, and more have been known to trot around the park (with their bodyguards). To find out if any filmmakers are in Savannah, the *Savannah Morning News* offers an outstanding Web site. Find www.savannahnow.com and check out the entertainment section of that newspaper on-line. (If you're intent on traveling to Savannah during production of a film, ask the entertainment writer directly for advice on when to come.)

BREAKFAST

Freshen up and head downstairs with your complimentary newspaper to the beautiful **Magnolia Cafe,** on the first floor of the hotel. This cheerful, intimate eatery is set amid flourishing tropical greenery and is a great place to start your day. Now prepare to discover Savannah's treasures in quaint shops located just steps away.

Remember your jog around Forsyth Park? Well, head in that same direction and at any street between the hotel and the park, turn west and walk a block to Whitaker Street. This one-way two-lane road is busy, so cross carefully and, as the merchants along this enchanting sidewalk say, "Walk on Whitaker between Jones and Taylor Streets." This tiny shopping district has the feel of a European city with its classic Savannah architecture, colorful characters and shop owners, fresh lemonade and delightful snacks, and adorable galleries and shops.

The **Bothwell Gallery** (422 Whitaker Street; 888–631–2259) is noted by its checkered moon that hangs just outside the door.

Enter and you'll find regional artwork, jewelry, and unique furniture. The shop is open Monday through Saturday, 10:30 A.M. to 5:30 P.M. Nearby, you'll find **Off the Wall** (412 Whitaker Street; 912–233–8840), a gallery featuring contemporary art and jewelry, sculpture, art books, dolls, and journals. Owner Gail Levites will welcome you Savannah-style!

Don't miss **Walsh Mountain Ironworks** (417 Whitaker Street; 912–239–9818), where Savannah's architecture is reflected in wrought-iron works. While she's not looking, purchase your sweetheart a wrought-iron light fixture that holds only candles as a romantic reminder of your Savannah visit. **One Fish, Two Fish** (405 Whitaker Street; 912–447–4600) is filled with cottage furniture, garden fancies, and decorative objects.

DAY TWO: afternoon

LUNCH

Shopping has made you hungry, so after you've left your purchases in your room at the hotel, walk east down Liberty 1 block to Abercorn Street and head south. A secret little restaurant has opened and has become a downtown resident's dream! **Good Eats** (606 Abercorn Street; 912–447–5444; moderate) is an adorable cafe that offers what they call "eclectic cuisine." Select a window seat for two and dine on spiral pasta and seasoned shrimp tossed with a fresh basil pesto. Divine! Or try the blackened yellowfin tuna served with a lemon thyme butter sauce and topped with a mango and Vidalia onion chutney. Whatever you do, don't forget to order a plate of hot, spicy biscuits to feed your mate! (And if you can discreetly take one home, do so!)

As they say on the big screen, "that's a wrap," so check out of the hotel and feel comforted knowing that reliving your two-day stay in this Oscar-loving city is only a video rental away!

ᗷad to the ᗷone

SAVANNAH'S WILD SIDE

EELING FRISKY? THEN LET YOUR HAIR DOWN—get down-and-dirty and walk on the wild side. Savannah can be a bit sleazy, and sometimes that's fun. Buy a pair of leather pants and find the nearest disco and dance until the sun comes up. Then soar above the city in a hot-air balloon and speed away on a Jet Ski. This slow-moving city-by-the-sea can be racy if you know where to go. Follow this script for a wild time in Savannah.

PRACTICAL NOTES: For this itinerary inhibition should be left at home and a spirit of adventure should prevail. But to set you up for your walk on the wild side, you'll be staying in a den of luxury, not a den of iniquity! You'll spend your first afternoon and early evening being pampered and relaxing before your late night out, so bring some fancier resort duds for the first part of your stay. For the more daring activities, bring plenty of cash (it costs money to break new ground) and pack your best pair of worn jeans, some rubber-soled, waterproof boating shoes, and a bathing suit.

DAY ONE: afternoon

Get wild in your room at the **Westin Savannah Harbor Resort** (1 Resort Drive; 912–201–2000). For a one-night stay, choose the Golf and Spa Package ($258 per night), which includes a round of golf for one or a spa treatment at the resort's **Greenbrier Spa.** The spa treatment includes a soaking in the same mysterious sulphur

◆ Get ready to get wild in the **Westin Savannah Harbor Resort** *(1 Resort Drive, Hutchinson Island; 912–201–2000)! Sweat in the sauna of **The Greenbrier Spa** or challenge the links at an eighteen-hole golf course surrounded by salt marshes.*

◆ *Dine in an elegant restaurant,* **Aquastar,** *located inside the Westin. It overlooks the city of Savannah and its bustling river. Then catch a ferry over to River Street where the rock and roll is just warming up.*

◆ *Buy your baby some leather at* **Savannah Harley-Davidson** *(East River Street; 912–231–8000) and head over to* **Malone's** *(912–234–3059) in City Market to refuel. If you're still ready to go, check out* **Hip Huggers** *(9 West Bay Street; 912–233–6999).*

◆ *Up, up, and away you'll fly the next day. Rent a beautiful hot-air balloon from* **Feather Air of Savannah** *(912–858–2529) for an hour-long trip over the city.*

◆ *Lunch at one of Savannah's claims to fame,* **Williams Seafood** *(Highway 80 East; 912–898–9222).*

◆ *Bring your cameras to catch the look on your mate's face when the dolphins dance right up to the edge of the boat on a trip with* **Low Country River Excursions** *(Highway 80 East; 912–898–9222).*

crystals that made the original Greenbrier in West Virginia famous, a Swiss shower spray (you're drenched with spray from sixteen shower heads), and a fifty-minute massage. If you choose golf as your diversion, ask your mate to chauffeur the golf cart and enjoy a tour of the golf course, framed by the magnificent Savannah River Bridge and surrounded by salt marshes and wildlife. Afterward, splurge with a pedicure for two (for an extra cost). Sip bottled water in the steam room and then dry off and head out to the hotel's pool, right on the waterfront. After a relaxing afternoon, return to your room to get ready for an evening of excitement.

DAY ONE: evening

DINNER

Start the evening watching the setting sun cast a golden hue over the Savannah riverfront. Reservations you made earlier in the day for the **Aquastar Restaurant** (inside the Westin; 1 Resort Drive, Hutchinson Island; 912–201–2000; moderate to expensive) should include a window-front table. With an open-air kitchen and casual atmosphere, this restaurant serves up an elegant dinner. For starters, try the blue crab drizzled with a lemon dill mustard aioli ($6.95), and ask your companion to share the "Colossal shrimp," hand-dipped in island rice-flour batter with a Cajun pepper aioli ($6.95). Entrees are divine, and the restaurant boasts many local favorites. Try River Street Flounder ($15.95), an almond-Parmesan encrusted fillet with a Dixie-style butter sauce and sour cream mashed potatoes. Savannah-style lobster is a dish you'll long remember. This lobster is stuffed to capacity with fresh crabmeat glazed with a tangy sauce and served with an old Southern favorite, country cheddar grits ($26.75). Treat your mate to a scoop or two of house-made Georgia peach ice cream before challenging the activity across the river. After dinner, change into something more casual and funky before you stroll down to the ferry dock just in front of the hotel and hop a vessel for a short ride across to River Street. The night is young, and wild Savannah is calling!

From the ferry landing, head east on River Street to **Savannah Harley-Davidson** (503 East River Street; 912–231–8000) and purchase some leather gear for your night out. The store offers a variety of Harley gifts, leather goods, and motor clothes. Then head back up the stairs and cross Bay Street to City Market. The bikes will be lining up, and the local Harley Club members will be hanging out and talking bikes. They're a friendly bunch of young to retired Savannahians who like to have fun, and if you ask, they'll show you their bikes for no charge. (Just don't touch!)

Though live music fills the air, resist the urge to hang out in the City Market courtyard with the after-work crowd. This is your night to get crazy. By 10:00 P.M., the crowd will be spinning on the sidewalks directly in front of the bandstand. You two are up for some action not quite so tame. Exit the steamy night air and pop in to **Malone's** (City Market; 27 Barnard Street; 912–234–3059) for some dirty dancing. There's a lighted disco floor upstairs, but if you're too timid to test it, stay downstairs. You can climb onto a bar stool and sip a frozen drink selected from a wall-size menu (try "190 Octane" for potency). You'll almost certainly run into reporters from the

Savannah Morning News, who hang out there, so now's your chance to do something that'll make the headlines.

Wow 'em and leave 'em gaping. It's getting late, so walk down Bay Street and stop off at other clubs along the way, if you dare. **Hip Huggers** (9 West Bay Street; 912–233–6999; inexpensive) is one you might try (don't worry about breaking curfew). It's too late to catch the ferry back, so call Yellow Cab (912–236–1133) and take a dreamy ride over the illuminated cable-span bridge back to the Westin. Your bed will be turned down, making it easy for you and your mate to hit the sheets and get wild.

DAY TWO: morning

BREAKFAST

Your love is in the clouds today (or will be, soon) as you share breakfast in a hot-air balloon. Leave the city and take I–16 toward Macon. Exit at the town of Black Creek; the drive will take you about twenty-five minutes from downtown. **Feather Air of Savannah** (off I–16, next to Black Creek Golf Course; 912–858–2529) is located on a picturesque plot of farmland where an old Victorian home stands. When you call to make your prior arrangements, you can request either the sunshine yellow or Savannah sky–blue balloon. This morning your pilot will bring along orange juice and pastries as you float above the world. If you're looking for a truly romantic way to propose, the balloon can be equipped with roses and champagne. The sixty-minute ride takes you over the marshlands and farms of this south Georgia town. The cost is $150 per person (cash only).

DAY TWO: afternoon

LUNCH

When you land, return to your car and take the scenic route down the Islands Expressway toward Tybee Island. Turn left just before you reach the Bull River Bridge. **Williams Seafood** (8010 East Highway 80; 912–897–2219; inexpensive), your next stop, is on your left, and Bull River Marina is on your right.

The Williamses' story is one of love and perseverance; as you near this humble establishment, share this story with your companion. It was 1936 and a hot, sultry summer along this stretch of two-lane road to Tybee Island. Tom Williams, a bridge tender for the Georgia State Highway Department, and his wife Leila, started selling fish and crabs that Tom had caught while tending the bridge. Their tiny table consisted of large pans of ice filled with the raw seafood. Savannahians going to and from the beach were thrilled to purchase fresh sea trout for ten cents a pound and boiled crabs for fifteen cents a dozen. One day, Mrs. Williams developed a special recipe for deviled crab, which she prepared from her home kitchen just steps away. She began selling her crabs—three for a quarter— and customers began to call her "Mom." As the business grew, they expanded their small roadside stand. A few years later, an old one-room structure across the highway became vacant. With three tables and an old kerosene stove, the couple served fried and boiled shrimp, fried fish, hush puppies, and of course, Leila's popular deviled crab. In the 1950s, the couple finally opened an official restaurant that began attracting hundreds daily. Today, the third generation of Williamses, Tommy and Carol, host seafood lovers in their new 500-seat restaurant.

Have a light lunch of shrimp salad and crab stew, then move right along to your next adventure.

Cross Highway 80 (directly in front of Williams) and park in the lot designated for marina guests. Walk down the dock to **Low Country River Excursions** (Bull River Marina, Highway 80 East; 912–898–9222), *the* place to go for afternoon thrills. (Now's the time to get rid of those street clothes! The dock offers two rest rooms with showers for changing.) Two can hop aboard a Jet Ski— provided their combined weight is 300 pounds or less—for $30 for a half hour and $50 for an hour (plus a required $200 deposit, made by credit card, for damages you might incur; the deposit is refunded when the Jet Ski is returned in good condition). Grab the waist of your love and hang on! A few spins up and down the Bull River will bring on the screams!

After you turn your Jet Ski in, Low Country River Excursions is still standing by—this time to slow the pace a bit. Your screams will turn to squeals of delight as you experience another sort of wildlife—the dolphins, salt marshes, and mud flats of the Bull River. The captain will take you wherever you want to go, and prices will vary according to the length of your excursion. You can opt for a tour that will take you around Wilmington Island on a 40-foot-long covered pontoon boat, where you'll view plantation-like homes along the waterfront. Or you can learn about native inhabitants such as the egrets, herons, and ospreys on a ninety-minute creek tour. The seasonal excursions are available from March 1 through November 30, so you can be sure it will tie in nicely with your other wild fair-weather adventures.

For MORE ROMANCE

Wild nights are calling at the **Bayou Cafe** (14 North Abercorn Street; 912–233–6411), where the crowd gets rowdy after 10:00 P.M. Hold on! You can feel the floor shake when things get moving at this club, an old cotton warehouse above River Street.

Soothing the Savage Beast

THE SAVANNAH SYMPHONY

NOTHING IS QUITE SO STIMULATING as a live performance of music. Savannah boasts a professional orchestra—the Savannah Symphony—rated "Best in the State" in 1995 (with competition from Atlanta and Augusta) by the Georgia Council of the Arts. The group comprises nearly forty full-time musicians and a host of other professionals who participate in the season, which begins in September and ends in May. String quartets, brass ensembles, and both a Masterworks Program and a Pops Program will please every taste. In addition, each season the group invites celebrity performers and musicians to share its stage. Dudley Moore, Carol Channing, and Itzhak Perlman are among the well-known guest artists who have appeared here.

PRACTICAL NOTES: To plan this elaborate night on the town, you will need to hire a private carriage to take you to dinner, to the concert hall, and out for coffee. You'll also need to call ahead to the Savannah Symphony Orchestra office (225 Abercorn Street; 912–236–9536) for a schedule of its 300-plus concerts a year. Lastly, make reservations for dinner.

DAY ONE: afternoon

You may want to sing for joy when you check into your room at the **Manor House** (201 West Liberty Street; 912–233–9597; $145 to

Romance AT A GLANCE

◆ Delight in the hospitality you'll receive at **The Manor House Inn** *(201 West Liberty Street; 912–233–9597), the perfect place to stay for your symphonic rendezvous.*

◆ *Ride in a horse-drawn carriage to the contemporary elegance of* **The Sapphire Grill** *(Congress Street; 912–443–9962) and dine in an intimate cove on the second floor.*

◆ *Have your carriage driver take you to an evening of classical music performed by the Savannah Symphony at the* **Johnny Mercer Theatre** *(Montgomery and Liberty Streets; 912–651–6556).*

◆ *If the night is still young for you and your mate, toast your grand evening in Savannah at the* **Pink House Tavern** *(23 Abercorn Street; 912–232–4286).*

$225), adjacent to the Civic Center. Perched high above Liberty Street, this recently refurbished inn offers five richly decorated and spacious suites that adjoin lavish parlors. Built in 1830, the Manor House was once a part of the Ballastone Inn and is owned and operated by the former Ballastone owner, Dick Carlson, a master of hospitality. Three of the suites include whirlpool baths and fresh terry-cloth robes; many of the suites are romantic enough to keep you entertained without leaving the premises.

An evening in Savannah! It's the perfect excuse to spend the afternoon shopping for a special night out. Treat each other to alluring attire. **Gaucho** (250 Bull Street; 912–232–7414) is good for women's clothing that is both unique and classy. For gentlemen who really want to put on the dog, tuxedo rentals can be arranged through the inn, or call **Simon's Formal Wear** (Oglethorpe Mall; 912–352–1251).

DAY ONE: evening

DINNER

Carriage Tours of Savannah (912–236–6756; $65 per hour Sunday through Thursday, $85 per hour Friday and Saturday) will send a carriage to your inn for a leisurely ride to dinner at the **Sapphire Grill** (110 West Congress Street; 912–443–9962; expensive), an upscale restaurant located near City Market in the heart of the Historic District. Call ahead for reservations at the Sapphire, then ask your carriage driver to allow you at least ninety minutes to enjoy the restaurant's refreshing array of Southern cuisine. Housed in a typical Savannah brick-walled building, this establishment, with metal accents and contemporary furnishings throughout, is one of the most intimate eateries in the city. Ask for the most seductive seat in the house—a single table located in a small enclave on the second floor.

Appetizers range from $5.00 to $13.00 and include crab and lobster cakes, fried green tomatoes, flash-seared tuna medallions, and James Island littleneck clams. The fried calamari glazed with preserved ginger is another outstanding appetizer, so plan to exchange plates during this part of the meal.

The artfully presented entrees include a luscious, crispy lemon benne black grouper with coriander whipped potatoes and soy-glazed, wok-seared vegetables. For dessert try the Sapphire Sundae, a bowl of fresh berries and sorbet, and a steaming cup of cappuccino.

Small Pleasures

Steps away from the bustling Savannah River, follow the ballastone street to the **All-American Popcorn Company, Inc.** *(427 East River Street; 912–236–3847; inexpensive). Ask the owner, Bert, to serve you and your companion a slice of homemade pizza (large enough for two to share) or a deli-style sandwich on freshly baked bread. Or wash down a Boar's Head hot dog with freshly squeezed lemonade. This tiny eatery seats thirty people; if weather permits, you can dine outside. (Better take along a dollar bag of popcorn when you leave, to cure the late-night munchies.) Open Monday through Saturday 11:00 A.M. to 11:00 P.M., Sunday noon to 7:00 P.M.*

After dinner have your driver take you to the **Johnny Mercer Theatre** at the Savannah Civic Center (Montgomery and Liberty Streets; 912–651–6556) for the concert. Single tickets range from $17.50 to $48.50 for Masterworks performances and from $15 to $40 for Pops performances. Dress runs the gamut from casual to formal, so you should feel comfortable in any attire. But if you

Johnny Mercer

As you walk along the streets of Savannah, you shouldn't be surprised to hear someone humming a bar or two of "Moon River," or "Ac-Cent-Tchu-Ate the Positive." The words to these famous songs and many others—including "Hooray for Hollywood!"—were written by Savannah-born Johnny Mercer. Born in 1909, this famous lyricist gave eloquent meaning to the melodies of composers from Hoagy Carmichael to Henry Mancini. Leaving Savannah in the 1920s, Mercer moved to New York to pursue acting. He did not, however, forget his hometown or the banks of the Vernon River, where he received inspiration for his lyrics during frequent vacation trips home.

In 1935 Mercer's radio show—Johnny Mercer's Music Shop—was a hit. And in 1942 Mercer helped found Capitol Records. Mercer won Oscars for "In the Cool, Cool, Cool of the Evening," "On the Atchison Topeka and Santa Fe," and for Mancini's "Moon River" and "The Days of Wine and Roses." Today Savannahians hum the music to his tunes, which received renewed popularity thanks to Clint Eastwood's film Midnight in the Garden of Good and Evil.

All around the city there are pleasant reminders of Mercer. There is the theater named for him; there is a tree-lined boulevard on neighboring Wilmington Island that pays tribute to him; and on some weeknights at Hannah's East and Chadwick's, his lyrics are brought to life by Miss Emma Kelly (Mercer's "Lady of 6,000 Songs"), who plunks and croons his tunes long after the sun sets on Savannah. When you visit Savannah, prepare to be romanced by reminders of a legend who wrote melodiously about love.

choose to arrive in your new stylish apparel, you'll fit right in with music-savvy Savannahians.

When the show is over, ask your driver to clip-clop over to the romantic **Planters Tavern,** inside the Olde Pink House Restaurant (23 Abercorn Street; 912–232–4286; inexpensive), where two large brick fireplaces will entice you in for a nightcap or a cup of espresso. A jazz pianist performs Tuesday through Sunday evenings, and the atmosphere is quiet and romantic, an ideal finale to a symphonic evening on the town.

Return to your carriage and take a last turn through the streets of Savannah on the way back to Manor House. Before turning in, indulge in the chocolates and brandy left in your room, and plan for your next melodious rendezvous.

For More Romance

Renew your vows or recite them the first time in one of Savannah's beautiful squares. Traditionally, **Whitfield Square** (located south on Habersham Street, between East Gordon and East Taylor Streets), with its white gazebo, has been favored as a wedding site. The **Fragrant Garden** (in Forsyth Park), renovated in 1990 and landscaped for small parties and weddings, is another popular wedding setting. Equipped with running water and electricity, the garden boasts its own private fountain and is separated from the park by a locked gate.

Before you say "I do," you must first contact the **City of Savannah Park and Tree Department** (912–651–6610) for permission to use the area you desire. The time limit for a park wedding is two to three hours, and cleanup is your responsibility. Couples who want musical accompaniment must apply for a separate permit from the city manager's office for any type of amplified sound. Applicants are accepted on a first-come, first-served basis and should call as early as possible to reserve a date.

In the Pink
A Garden, a House—and Pigs!

FOLLOW YOUR HEARTS TO SAVANNAH in springtime when a floral wonderland unfolds and a magical palette of pastel colors inspires a passionate and fulfilling respite. Spring, and its promise of renewal, is everywhere—from tiny Southern eateries and fine, historic restaurants to the sidewalks of the Historic District and the tree-lined paths and magnificent gardens of Forsyth Park. This itinerary will help your love blossom again. The afterglow will be eternal.

PRACTICAL NOTES: This itinerary is recommended for springtime, when Savannah's world-renowned splendor is at its peak. But as surely as spring comes to Savannah, so do seasonal sniffles. Parks and roadways are lined with blooming azaleas, so bring along plenty of tissues and allergy medication in case this parade of blossoms rubs your noses the wrong way. It's an extra busy time, so be extra sure to call ahead for reservations at Magnolia Place. Bryan's Pink Pig Bar-B-Q does not accept reservations; the Olde Pink House Restaurant requires them.

DAY ONE: morning

To take advantage of a whole glorious spring day together, arrive in downtown Savannah early in the day and drop your bags at one of the city's finest historic inns. From the verandas of the **Magnolia Place Inn** (503 Whitaker Street; 912–236–7674 or 800–238–7674; $140 to $265), lucky guests can peer through the palm branches and watch Forsyth Park come to life each morning. Among the pink azaleas, locals walk their dogs, joggers lope around the park's pathways, and

Romance AT A GLANCE

♦ Sit on the front porch and partake of the varying shades of pink all around **The Magnolia Place Inn** (503 Whitaker Street; 912–236–7674). Forsyth Park lies just ahead and the view of that magnificent fountain from your rocking chair is the best in the city!

♦ Spend the morning lying about on the grassy lawn of the park, then drive over the cable-span bridge to the tiny town of Bluffton.

♦ Share the romance of soul food with your soul mate at **Bryan's Pink Pig Bar-B-Q** (Highway 17A, Levy, S.C.; 843–784–3635).

♦ Take a horse-drawn carriage to **The Olde Pink House** (23 Abercorn Street; 912–232–4286) for dinner and drinks afterward at the tavern below.

♦ Spend some time enjoying the sound of spring, then walk through the streets of Savannah and partake of the beauty of the season!

squirrels scurry about on the lawn. This bright and airy inn is one of Savannah's more popular—you won't need rose-colored glasses to view its full magnificence. All fifteen rooms are original to the house, and the foyer's unusual parquet floor and wainscoting are also original. The expansive foyer leads to a superbly decorated parlor, and an impressive staircase will lead you to your plush room (when it becomes available at the 2:30 P.M. check-in time). Request one of the two upstairs front rooms (the General Joseph Warren Room or the General Nathanael Greene Room); both open out onto the bowed porch of this 1878 Victorian mansion. Elegantly furnished with period antiques and complete with Jacuzzi baths and working fireplaces in most rooms, the Magnolia Place Inn is also the birthplace of author Conrad Aiken and, ironically, housed another literary success, John Berendt, during his stay in Savannah for the writing of *Midnight in the Garden of Good and Evil*. Purchase Aiken's book *Selected Poems*, which won the Pulitzer Prize in 1930. The author once said, "In a way, I never stopped writing about Savannah." Read his eloquent words aloud to your companion, then set out to see the city.

All couples will look pretty in pink against the springtime flowers, so you two should head outdoors to enjoy the morning at **Forsyth Park,** named for John Forsyth: governor, U.S. senator, and secretary of state from 1834 to 1841.

The northern end of this twenty-six-acre spread is graced by

Blind Love

Savannah's illustrious **Forsyth Park** is filled with romance, as not only the sights but also the scents are alluring. Aside from the ornate fountain created in 1858, there's the Fragrant Garden for the Blind, a place where the scent of flowers can paint a picture of beauty for those who can't see. Blindfold your partner and go astray in this aromatic garden, then play hide-and-seek amid the illustrious oak trees lining the park's pathways.

unique fountains, statues, and benches in grassy areas. White, pink, and purple flora, splendid live oaks, and a mixture of tropical palm trees make this the perfect setting for both weddings and proposals. (If you decide to wed here, contact the **City of Savannah Park and Tree Department** for rules and regulations; 912–651–6610.)

The southern part of the park has a busier ambience. Once the drill field and parade ground of the Savannah Militia, this section features monuments honoring military events and heroes. Most of these pay tribute to the Confederacy (which was lost twice to the British and once to the Union) or to Georgians who served in the Civil War and Spanish-American War. Among the latter are General Lafayette McLaws and Brigadier General Francis S. Bartow (who led Savannah troops and was killed at the Battle of Bull Run in 1861). Here too are tennis courts, a playground, and other areas for active pursuits like softball and Ultimate Frisbee.

Spread a blanket on the northern lawns and tell each other your daydreams, or walk to the south end of the park to play a set or two of tennis. If you're thirsty, try a fresh fruit smoothie or a gourmet decaf from the **Brighter Day Natural Foods** (1102 Bull Street; 912–236–4703; inexpensive), a Savannah favorite for healthy noshing.

DAY ONE: afternoon

LUNCH

Slothful bliss may have been your choice for at least a part of the morning, but you've probably worked up somewhat of an appetite exploring the park. A short drive over the Savannah River Bridge to Alternate Highway 17 near Bluffton, South Carolina, will bring even more delight to your pink itinerary. Follow the road until you see, on your right, the bright pink pig hovering over a hand-painted sign that reads RESTAURANT. Park in front of the cinder-block building with flying pink pigs painted all over its exterior and prepare to learn the meaning of the phrase "Hog Heaven."

Bryan's Pink Pig Bar-B-Q (Highway 17A, Levy, S.C.; no phone; inexpensive) is one of those rare finds that connoisseurs of true Southern down-home cuisine often keep to themselves. You won't find it on a list of "Must Sees and Must Dos" in travel stories about Savannah, and, after you've sampled the fare, you won't want to share your discovery with too many friends. It might soon become too popular.

Inside, winged ceramic pigs dangle from every inch of the ceiling, and lacy, floral cloths adorn each table. Take a window booth for two and tell the waitress you want to sample the barbecue and ribs described as a buffet on the hot-pink menu. For a mere $7.00 for chopped barbecue and $9.00 for ribs, you'll be filled to the brim, but leave room for the best peach cobbler on the East Coast. Be sure to sample the sweetened iced tea, and prepare to pay with cash (that's all they accept here). Hours are 11:00 A.M. to 4:00 P.M. Tuesday, 11:00 A.M. to 7:00 P.M. Wednesday, and 11:00 A.M. to 8:00 P.M. Thursday through Saturday for a seafood sampler. As you waddle out to your car feeling like a pair of stuffed pink pigs, feel sorry for the droves of people back in Savannah who are still standing in line for lunch at the city's most popular eateries.

Drive back to Savannah and claim both your bags and the gorgeous room you booked at Magnolia Place. After a nap, step out on your private tree-shaded veranda for an afternoon glass of wine as downtown working Savannahians travel Whitaker Street to their homes on the south side.

DAY ONE: evening

DINNER

Around 7:30 P.M. call **Carriage Tours of Savannah** (10 Warner Street; 912–236–6756) and have them pick you up for dinner at the **Olde Pink House Restaurant** (23 Abercorn Street; 912–232–4286;

expensive). Once called the Habersham House, the 1771 structure mysteriously began to earn its new name when the original bricks started to bleed through the plastered walls and change the color of the building from white to "Jamaican pink."

The Georgian mansion housing the restaurant was built on land granted by the Crown of England, and James Habersham Jr. lived here from 1771 to 1800. The site of many secret meetings held to secure the independence of the thirteen colonies from England, the Pink House was transformed in 1811 into the Planter's Bank, the first bank in Georgia. The former bank vaults are still used today, as wine cellars. In 1992 the William Balish family of Charleston purchased the house and restored it to its present-day elegance. Diners frequently report sightings of ghosts, and candles have been said to relight themselves on the mantel of the dining rooms downstairs. Fresh seafood, lamb, and duck are regular menu items, and desserts are extravagant.

Have a Cow!

Don't pig out—dine where the food is udderly delicious. The owner of the **606 Cafe** (319 West Congress Street; 912–236–5113) is moooved by cows, and the restaurant is overflowing with dangling udders and other bovine motifs. Those who crave raw or steamed seafood may sit out on the Cow Patio and peel fresh shrimp to the rhythm of a live guitarist. Those romantics with udder interests may prefer to dine indoors in a private alcove encased by beads and accented with dangling bras, corsets, and pantyhose. In either setting, your meal is bound to be memorable.

Once you've completed your meal, exit and descend the stairs to the delightful ambience of the **Planter's Tavern.** Gail Thurmond, a local vocalist and pianist, will treat you to standards by Mercer and Mancini as she plays quietly (nightly, except Monday) to a very upscale crowd. As the fireplace beckons you to linger, do just that. The atmosphere is guaranteed to provide the perfect nightcap for your pastel-colored day.

DAY TWO: morning

BREAKFAST

On the front porch of your room at the Magnolia, sip fresh orange juice and enjoy fresh fruit, pastries, or homemade quiche.

The city is bursting with color, so don't linger too long. Call Carriage Tours of Savannah and request the downtown historic district tour that best offers garden sites. The horse-drawn carriage will allow you a pleasing, street-level view of the flowers in the coolness of the morning. Ask your guide to pass Forsyth Park, one of the best places to view the city's floral glory.

Your tour ends in City Market. Stroll over to Johnson Square (2 blocks east on Congress Street) and walk 3 blocks east to Habersham Street. Head south down Habersham for lunch.

DAY TWO: afternoon

LUNCH

Savor the charm of a quaint, Savannah eatery, the **Voo Doo Cafe** (321 Habersham Street; 912–447–1999; moderate). Dine outdoors if the weather permits it. If you dine indoors, sit by the window. Fresh flowers adorn the tables and the food is purely Savannah. Though it changes daily, the menu always includes deliciously fresh salads, topped with fruit, cheese, nuts, or seafood. The cafe is open daily from 8:00 A.M. to 3:30 P.M.

From Habersham Street, head south until you reach picturesque Victory Drive, its median lined with palms interspersed with blazing azaleas and delicate dogwoods. Take a right onto Victory and continue to Abercorn Street, the main avenue of one of Savannah's most aristocratic neighborhoods. Head south on Abercorn, and after a fifteen- to twenty-minute drive, you'll reach I–95. Your pink idyll is ended.

FOR MORE ROMANCE

Savannah is a floral wonderland during spring, so it's no wonder that the Garden Club of Savannah hosts its annual **NOGS Tour of Hidden Gardens** when everything seems in bloom. At least eight private gardens are open for public viewing; the garden of the Massie Heritage Center is also shared. The two-day affair additionally offers a chance to enjoy a "Simply Southern Tea" at the Sculpture Gallery of the Telfair Museum of Art. Call (912) 238–0248 for more information.

Another popular springtime event is **Night in Old Savannah,** which is usually held the same weekend as the garden tour. Presented by and benefiting the Coastal Heritage Society, its theme varies from year to year, and well-known entertainers highlight the weekend of eating beneath the skies. Held at the Historic Railroad Shops, the event features a variety of foods, including raw oysters and barbecue sandwiches; gates open at 6:30 P.M. and the event concludes at midnight. For specific dates and admission information, call (912) 651–6823.

$\mathcal{S}$plendor in the $\mathcal{G}$rass

A PICNIC—AND MORE—IN RICHMOND HILL

AVE A FLING IN A SECLUDED OUTDOOR MANSION made by nature—walls of live oak and a ceiling of sunlit sky. In Richmond Hill, a trendy suburb of Savannah, you can spend the day lying in the cool shade munching on delicacies while the world passes by on nearby I–95. Because of its proximity to the waterfront, Richmond Hill has attracted the wealthy, who have built beautiful homes in this attractive suburb.

Surrounding the community are thick woodlands interspersed with beautiful rivers and marshlands—the perfect setting for a playful afternoon.

PRACTICAL NOTES: Bring along the essentials for this day trip: a cooler filled with drinks, a blanket for picnicking, and a picnic lunch. Picnic fixin's may be purchased at Carey Hilliard's in Savannah or at Richmond Hill's Piggly Wiggly food market (Highway 144, Richmond Hill). Insect repellent is also advisable.

DAY ONE: morning

Leaving Savannah, drive south down Abercorn and stop at **Carey Hilliard's** (11111 Abercorn Street; 912–925–3225; inexpensive) for picnic food—maybe some shrimp-salad sandwiches, cole slaw, and homemade potato salad. Or, if you prefer, fill your picnic basket after you reach Richmond Hill (see DAY ONE: Afternoon).

Romance AT A GLANCE

♦ Enjoy divine salt marshes, bountiful wildlife, and an intriguing museum on a day trip to Richmond Hill.

♦ Feast on Southern fare for breakfast at **Hill Billiards** (Ford Plaza Shopping Center, Highway 144, Richmond Hill; 912–756–2479).

♦ Visit the **Richmond Hill History Museum** (Highway 144, Richmond Hill; 912–756–3697) where Henry Ford exhibits will take you back to the early days of the automobile.

♦ Purchase picnic supplies from the neighborhood Piggly Wiggly (Highway 44; 912–727–2339) and follow the shade trees for an afternoon of lying about at **Fort McAllister.**

Continue south on Abercorn until you reach I–95. Join the throngs heading south to Florida, but instead of following them, take the exit at Highway 144, about 5 miles from Savannah, and follow the signs straight into Richmond Hill (a three- to four-minute drive from I–95).

BREAKFAST

Join the locals for a "far from fancy" breakfast and a little local color at **Hill Billiards** (Ford Plaza Shopping Center, Highway 144, Richmond Hill; 912–756–2479; inexpensive). Eggs, bacon, grits, and biscuits are specialties here, along with talk of the local crops, economy, and politics. This is a true diner that will take you back a few years and put you in a nostalgic mood for your visit to this historic town.

Next stop is the **Richmond Hill Historical Society and Museum** (Highway 144, Richmond Hill; 912–756–3697), where docent Judy Paster will guide you through this quaint museum. You may be surprised to learn that the small city was founded by billionaire Henry Ford, who purchased more than 86,000 acres of Bryan County in the 1920s. Attracted to the area's mild climate, Ford utilized his space here to experiment with agricultural products that would one day assist him in modernizing the automobile industry. You'll see a sample case with original items (like a crest of an automobile from the 1920s) used on sales calls by Ford salesmen. And then there's the pair of socks that Ford, in his experimental mode, created from Richmond Hill sweet gum trees. Photographs of the old Ford Plantation capture its lavish parties, and a romantic etching shows Mr. and Mrs. Ford dancing on the front lawn of their Richmond Hill home. Today, the museum is the liveliest place to experience the plantation days. (The Ford home still remains; however, the land around it will become a housing development.) The museum is open from 10:00 A.M. to 5:00 P.M. daily. Donations are accepted in lieu of admission.

If you didn't buy picnic fixin's in Savannah, head over to the **Piggly Wiggly** food market (Highway 144; 912–727–2339) and buy some freshly made sandwiches, salads, fruit, sweets, or whatever strikes your fancy. Then follow the signs downtown to **Fort McAllister,** where a tree-lined drive will take you to a 1,700-acre park. Aside from its seductive arboreal attributes, the park is imbued with a historical flavor. On the site is one of the most well-preserved earthworks fortifications built during the Civil War by the Confederacy. It managed to withstand several attacks by Union warships, then was finally overtaken in 1864, marking the end of General William T. Sherman's March to the Sea. (The site was later owned by Henry Ford, before it was purchased by the state.)

The fort is open for leisurely, self-guided tours, so stay as long as you wish, studying the weapons and other Civil War relics. The hours are 9:00 A.M. to 5:00 P.M. Tuesday through Saturday and 2:00 to 5:30 P.M. on Sunday. Admission is $1.00 per person.

DAY ONE: afternoon

LUNCH

After you've refought the war in the fort, make your way to the recreational area where swings are shaded by live oaks and a wonderful picnic ground parallels the Ogeechee River. Tables, grills, and lots of sunny sites for spreading a blanket are available here. Open your picnic hamper and enjoy your lunch, then take a nap in the shade or the sun. When you awaken, take the back road (Highway 17) back to Savannah.

DAY ONE: evening

DINNER

Find love on the way back to Savannah at **Love's Seafood Restaurant** (Highway 17 South; 912–925–3616; moderate), a favorite waterfront spot where the hush puppies are habit-forming and fried catfish is the specialty. Sit by the window at sunset and watch the recreational boaters return to the public dock nearby. They'll be sunburned and you'll be cool as you place your order. Prepare to overeat. You'll be so sated when you leave you'll need to turn the volume up on the radio to help keep you awake.

FOR MORE ROMANCE

Word has it that Mr. Ford became so fond of sweets from a Savannah bakery that he moved the baker and his goods to Richmond Hill. When Ford's duties called him to Dearborn, Michigan, he'd have Amtrak's *Silver Meteor* stop by Richmond Hill for a box of sweets from the bakery. The baker's son is still in business—now in Claxton, Georgia—running the **Georgia Fruitcake Company**. Have a fruitcake delivered to your love as a fond remembrance of the picnic you shared among the pines and live oaks at Fort McAllister. (Call the Georgia Fruitcake Company at 912–739–2683).

General Index

Special Indexes

ROMANTIC RESTAURANTS

NIGHTLIFE

ROMANTIC ACCOMMODATIONS

TOURS

About the Author

GEORGIA R. BYRD IS A LIFELONG SOUTHERNER and seventeen-year resident of Savannah. Currently a writer and producer of publications, she was founding editor of *Savannah Magazine*. She also served as an editor, writer, and columnist for the *Savannah Morning News* and has written for other newspapers as well. Her articles have appeared in *Southern Living, Forbes, Atlanta Magazine,* and the *Atlanta Journal-Constitution*.

Georgia authored the Savannah chapter for the *1996 Insider's Guide to Atlanta* and is coauthor of the *History of Aviation in Savannah, Georgia,* and *Seasons of Savannah*.

She lives beside the marsh on an island with her husband; her children, Ammie and Whit Whitley; and their Jack Russell terrier, Snorkel.